Horseshoe Canyon Rock
Arkansas

Chad Watkins & Tom Hancock

Horseshoe Canyon Rock by Chad Watkins & Tom Hancock
© 2006 Boston Mountain Press, Inc.
All rights reserved. This book or any part thereof may not be reproduced in any form whatsoever, whether by graphic, visual, electronic, or any other means without written permission from Boston Mountain Press, Inc.

Published and distributed by
Boston Mountain Press, Inc.
1234 E. Meadowmere
Springfield, MO 65804
www.bostonmountainpress.com

ISBN-13: 978-0-9789409-0-4
ISBN-10: 0-9789409-0-3

Credit Info

Cover Photo: Zen Boulden on Lavender Eye by © Harrison Shull/Shullphoto
Inside Photo: Chad Davis on The Greatest Show on Earth by Tom Hancock
Back Photo: HCR Entrance by Tom Hancock
Route Drawings & Maps: Tom Hancock
Artwork courtesy of: © Jeremy Collins, www.jercollins.com
Cover Design: Katie Canada
Edited by: Amanda Smith

Printed in the USA by Litho Printers, Cassville, Missouri

WARNING: READ THIS BEFORE YOU USE THIS BOOK

Climbing is a very dangerous sport where you may be seriously injured or die. The information contained in this book is subjective and based entirely on opinions. This information may be incorrect or misleading. Many of the routes described in this book rely on fixed protection which may not be safe or may have been removed. Your safety depends on your own good judgment. Take all necessary precautions and evaluate your abilities honestly before attempting to climb a route described in this book. If you have any doubts, seek professional instruction and training.

THE AUTHORS AND PUBLISHER EXPRESSLY DISCLAIM ANY AND ALL WARRANTIES, EXPRESS OR IMPLIED, INCLUDING, BUT NOT LIMITED TO IMPLIED WARRANTIES OF MERCHANTABILITY AND FITNESS FOR A PARTICULAR PURPOSE. THE AUTHORS AND PUBLISHER EXPRESSLY DISCLAIM ANY AND ALL REPRESENTATIONS AND WARRANTIES REGARDING THIS GUIDE, THE ACCURACY AND RELIABILITY OF THE INFORMATION CONTAINED IN THIS GUIDE, AND THE RESULTS OF YOUR USE HEREOF. YOUR USE OF THIS BOOK INDICATES YOUR ASSUMPTION OF ALL RISKS ASSOCIATED WITH THE USE OF THIS GUIDE AND IS AN ACKNOWLEDGEMENT OF YOUR OWN SOLE RESPONSIBILITY FOR YOUR CLIMBING SAFETY.

Longtime bouldering visionary Justin Frese sends Trouser Chili

Acknowledgements

The climbs of Horseshoe Canyon and this resulting guidebook are a culmination of the efforts of many people who deserve recognition.

Without the Johnson family opening the Ranch to climbers, one of Arkansas' greatest climbing areas would not even exist. Their willingness to allow us to practice our craft in this day and age of lawsuit-paranoid landowners and their acceptance of our eccentric oddities has been a true blessing. For that, we all owe them the greatest of appreciation and respect.

From the early explorers who first discovered the rock climbing potential of Lick Hollow to today's steel-tendoned mutants, every first ascensionist deserves much praise for their hard work and efforts. Just who climbed what first will never truly be known, but among those who deserve special recognition for their climbing contributions are Carrie Allen, Jamie and McCree Anderson, Billy Bisswanger, Alf Carter, Chad and Mary Davis, Justin Frese, Clay Frisbie, Eric Hudkins, Rich McDade, Dave McGee, Tony Morris, Roger Raines, Chris Robertson, Jason Roy, Blake Strickland, Craig Thomas and Mike Wintroath. These climbers had the vision to help shape the climbing at the Ranch as it is today.

We would also like to thank Blake Strickland and Justin Frese for providing the information and mapping for the boulder problems. Their enthusiasm for the small rocks has brought Arkansas to the forefront of American bouldering.

This book would not have been possible without the technical support of Corey and Katie Canada, Jeremy Collins, Marty Jenkins, Jim Mayfield, Harrison Shull, Amanda Smith, and Blake Strickland.

Most importantly, we thank our lovely wives, Rhonda Watkins and Thesha Hancock, and our families for their inspiration and never-ending support for our sometimes time-consuming and ultimately unimportant hobby.

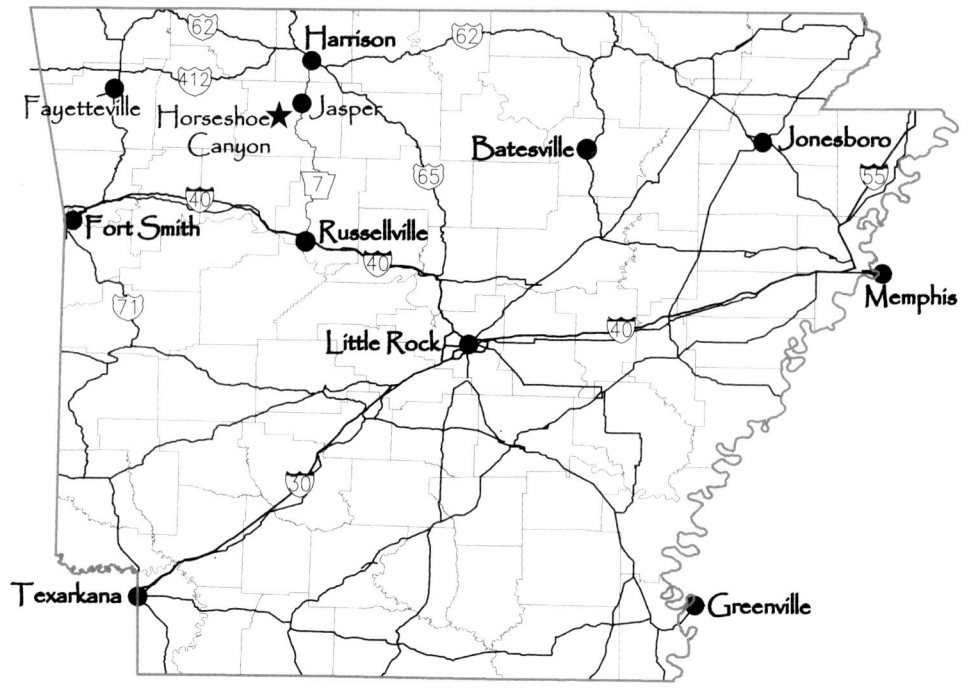

Welcome to the Ranch

It amazes me to think of the changes here since we first acquired the property in early 1995. I had been on the road working in sales and with a young and growing family was looking for a lifestyle change. My wife Amy and I had met working on a dude ranch outside Jackson hole, WY and I always thought that given the chance we'd love owning and running a guest ranch. We decided to take a shot and here we are.

I'd like to say I immediately recognized the climbing potential here, but climbing could not have been further from my mind. We loved the scenery and the big sandstone bluffs gave the Ranch a real western feel, but we never knew it possible to climb them or that it was so much dang fun. We have enjoyed watching the climbing take off here and appreciate all those who were a part of it. Chad, Jason, Tom and the early PETRA gang were all amazing, and their excitement and love of climbing shows in the work they did here on the Ranch and in the pages of this book. The friendships we have made and continue to make remind us why we're in this business to begin with.

Have fun, be safe, and remember this is my back yard so please be responsible and considerate of others.

Barry Johnson
Director of Operations
Horseshoe Canyon Ranch

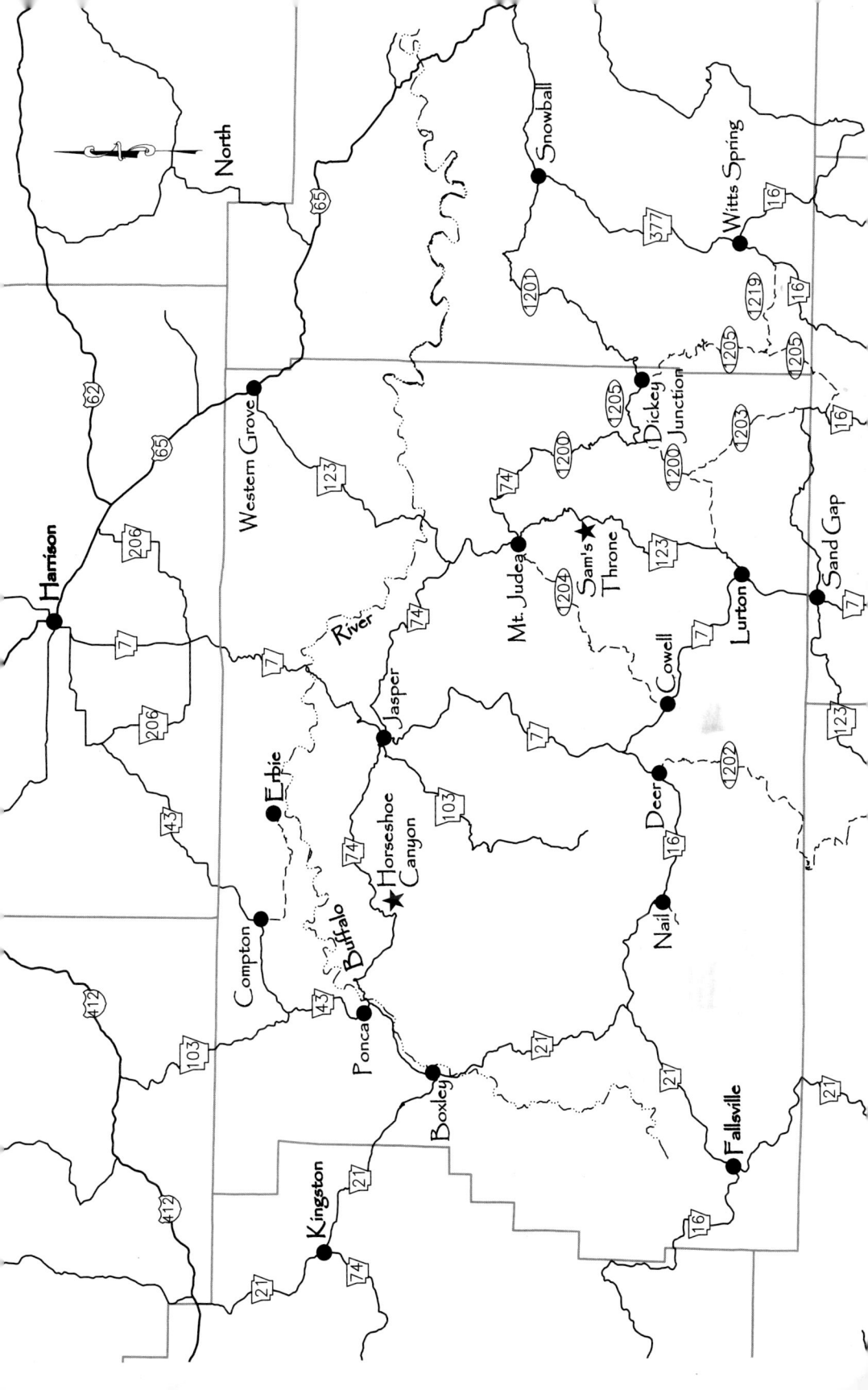

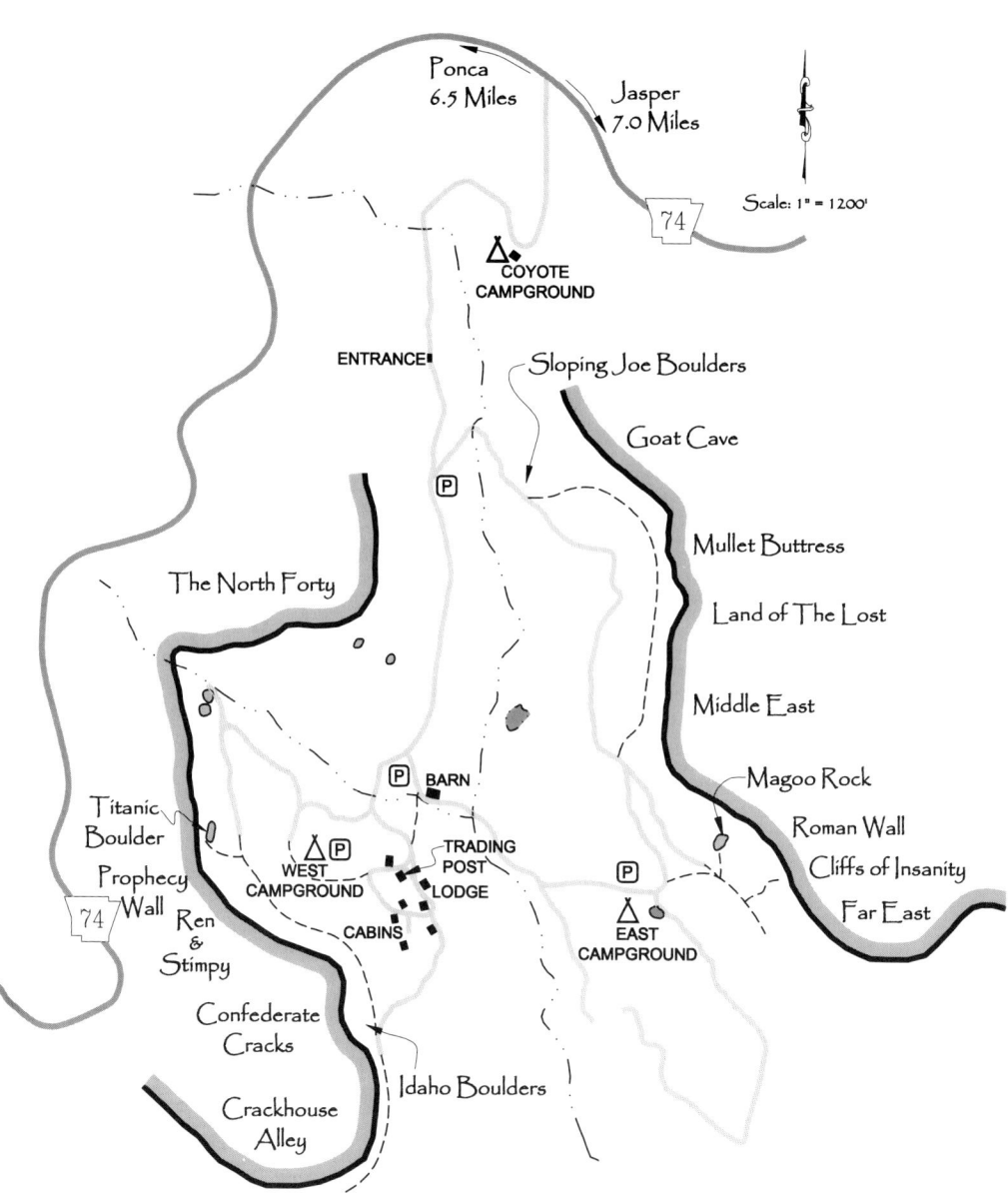

Overview Map

Table of Contents

FORWARD 9

INTRODUCTION 10

CRACKHOUSE ALLEY 14

SOUTH IDAHO BOULDERS 20

CONFEDERATE CRACKS 22

IDAHO BOULDERS 30

REN & STIMPY 32

THE PROPHECY WALL 36

THE TITANIC 40

THE NORTH FORTY 44

THE NORTH FORTY BOULDERS 58

THE GOAT CAVE 60

SLOPING JOE BOULDERS 65

MULLET BUTTRESS 66

LAND OF THE LOST 70

THE MIDDLE EAST 74

MAGOO ROCK 78

ROMAN WALL 82

CLIFFS OF INSANITY 86

THE FAR EAST 90

TICK LIST 96

ROUTE INDEX 100

Amanda Smith raising the standards on Lavender Eye

Forward

In the beginning, there was nothing… then we discovered caffeine, nicotine and rock! We are meant to climb, so we do. Throughout the evolution of climbing, from its bold beginnings with pioneers like Fritz Wiessner, John Gill, and Royal Robbins to the lycra clad spew-hounds of the Skinner days to the mutant invasion of the 90's, we have witnessed the many approaches one can take to climbing.

Among the more controversial of these approaches is sport climbing. The introduction of the bolt raised many eyebrows, "cuz bolts is cheatin'!" Despite this opposition, this new form of climbing allowed climbers to work harder moves and to do new routes that previously could not have been done safely. Subsequently, the "sport climber" was born.

To some extent, bolts are now accepted at almost every crag and in many walks of life: Buddhist, Christian, Pagan, and even the Republican. Specific "sport crags" have even popped up, the latest of which is Horseshoe Canyon Ranch.

With its acceptance of sport climbing, the Ranch has become the catalyst for pushing the standards of Arkansas climbing to new levels. This can be seen at the surrounding crags where climbers are applying their newfound power on previously unclimbed stone, and at the Ranch, where an increasing number of weekend warriors are sending 5.12.

Although the bolted climbs at the Ranch have firmly established sport climbing as an accepted style in Arkansas, they have also blurred the lines of what is considered acceptable at the surrounding crags. The manner in which every face climbing route has been completely bolted at the Ranch is not desirable at every crag. Arkansas has a fine tradition of naturally protected routes and it is just as important to continue pushing the mental standards as well as the physical. When establishing new routes in other areas, please keep this in mind.

Introduction

Horseshoe Canyon Ranch (HCR) offers some of the finest sandstone in Arkansas with nearly 250 routes ranging from 5.5 to 5.14. The majority of the routes are fully bolted sport climbs, but there are also many fine trad routes and a plethora of good boulder problems. The cracks at the Ranch are some of the best in Arkansas and will challenge even the saltiest of crack masters. Rest day activities include hiking, mountain biking, horseback riding, canoeing, and there is even an 18-hole Frisbee golf course. With instant appeal and beauty, the Ranch welcomes all who seek outdoor activity and is a great place to bring the whole family whether they like to climb or not.

Location & Directions

HCR is located approximately 7.0 miles west of Jasper and 6.5 miles east of Ponca on the south side of State Highway 74. Jasper is approximately 25 miles south of Harrison and 65 miles north of Russellville on Scenic State Highway 7.

Climate

The best time to climb at HCR is during the spring and fall, though winters are often equally pleasant on the south and west facing crags. Summer is generally quite hot and humid (not to mention the overabundance of ticks, chiggers, mosquitoes, poison ivy and snakes), but tolerable climbing can be found on the shadier faces.

Camping & Lodging

Primitive camping is available at HCR during the off-season (August 15th through May 15th) for $5 per person per day. Camping is permitted in designated areas only and campers are expected to camp with the utmost care and respect for the land and other campers.

Cabin rentals are also available during the off-season for a reduced rate and include showers, a kitchen area with microwave and refrigerator, and full access to the swimming pool and hot tub.

Year-round camping is available at The Coyote Campground (located at the white house at the top of the road just above HCR). Camping fees are $7 per person per night and include use of the shower house and cooking facilities. Breakfast is available for $5.

The nearest off-site camping can be found along the Buffalo National River at the Kyle's Landing or Steel Creek campgrounds, which can be reached by traveling either 3 miles east or 5 miles west of the HCR entrance on State Highway 74, respectively. Camping fees are currently $10 per site per night at these locations.

Hotel accommodations include Riverview and Gordon's, both located in Jasper. There are also numerous cabin rental options, so consult the area phone book or stop by the Chamber of Commerce on the north side of the square in Jasper.

Food & Supplies

The closest grocery stores and restaurants can be found in the town of Jasper. The Ozark Café, The Boardwalk Café, Sharon Kay's, and Pizza Pro are all located near the Jasper square. The Point of View is located ¼ mile west of Highway 7 on Highway 74. If you are looking for a real view of Ozark beauty while dining, The Cliff House Inn, located 7 miles south of Jasper on Highway 7, is a good choice. For all of these, you should call first to see if they are open.

Climbing Fees and Regulations

All climbers are required to register and pay a $5 daily climbing fee at The Trading Post, located along the main road near the cabins and lodge. First time users are also required to fill out and sign a liability waiver. The Trading Post will provide updated information on fees, road closures, camping, new route information, and upcoming events. Guide services, instruction, basic climbing equipment, supplies, and showers are also available at The Trading Post.

- "Leave No Trace." Pack out what you pack in, including toilet paper and food waste.
- Fires are only permitted in designating camping areas. Use only existing established fire rings. Thoroughly extinguish all campfires prior to leaving camp.
- Please be considerate of all horses and livestock.
- Pets are allowed but must be kept leashed and under control. The livestock and Anatolian shepherd dogs that guard the goats have hospitalized or killed more than one beloved pet.
- Do not approach or pet the Anatolian shepherd dogs.
- Do not play on or around the zip-lines or other high element structures. These are for HCR guests only and require HCR personnel supervision.
- If you are not a ranch guest, please stay out of the main lodge.
- Alcohol is not permitted around the bouldering or climbing areas.
- Foul language and disrespectful behavior will not be tolerated.
- Please do not cross property fences to access the outlying bluffs. Access on these privately owned cliffs is currently in a delicate state and must not be put in jeopardy.
- When toproping on the anchors, please use quickdraws or runners in lieu of running the rope directly through the rappel rings.
- Stay off the cliff tops and use existing anchors whenever possible.
- Climbing and camping at HCR is a privilege and HCR reserves the right to deny access to anyone for any reason.

Once again, for the adventurous types prone to wandering too far, climbing is not permitted outside the ranch boundaries. Property owners are increasingly aware of trespassing climbers and do not want anyone climbing on their property. Please respect the fences, for the other side is private property.

Ratings and Such

The difficulty ratings in this guidebook are based on the Yosemite Decimal System. This system generally grades the routes either by the single most difficult move on a route or the overall sustained nature. Because of this, a sustained 5.9 climb with every move a 5.9 may feel more difficult than a 5.10 with only one 5.10 move surrounded by a bunch of 5.7 climbing. As the difficulty of the climbs increases, the sustained nature of the climbing becomes more of a factor in the overall rating and a climb with sustained 5.11d climbing may garner a 5.12b rating over a climb with only a few 5.12a moves.

Though there have been many complaints that the ratings at the Ranch are not consistent, every attempt has been made to achieve a consensus on-sight lead climb rating for each route. Still, difficulty ratings are entirely subjective and not every climb will feel the same for each climber.

A route's difficulty rating may also be followed by a PG, R or X to provide some indication of the danger of a particular route. A route with a PG rating may have large runouts between protection where a fall may result in serious injury. R or X ratings usually indicate a significant lack of protection and that a fall could result in serious injury or death. All routes in this guidebook should be treated with respect whether or not they have a danger rating. Many of the easier routes rely on large holds that can and will break. A thirty foot fall is equally as dangerous from a 5.11 X as from an over-bolted 5.6.

To further confuse matters, the climbs have been given quality ratings, which are even more subjective. In general, each area will have a few routes that stand above the rest and are blessed with the coveted four-star rating. Also, routes established by one of the authors will receive at least one extra star. The routes with less stars are still worth doing and a climber may find a two-star route to be much better than a more popular four-star neighbor.

Believe it or not, bolt counts are also somewhat subjective. No matter how many times we counted them, certain routes always seemed to gain or lose a bolt. Regardless, the bolt counts at the end of each route description indicate the number of protection bolts on the climb but do not include the two anchor bolts at the top. It is usually wise to carry a few extra draws to be on the safe side.

New Routes

Though the majority of the plums have been picked, there is still room for more routes. If you would like to bolt a new route or put anchors on a crack you have done, please contact one of the ranch climbing guides first. In general, only stainless steel hangers and 1/2" x 3 ¾" stainless steel expansion or glue-in bolts may be used. The anchors should be specifically fabricated for rock climbing rather than using chains or other hardware store materials. If you don't know what you're doing, it will show in your work, and we will "fix it". If you have never bolted a route before, the Ranch is not the place to be learning, so NO FIRST-TIME BOLTERS please.

Bouldering

Though not covered extensively in this guidebook, the bouldering at the Ranch is outstanding and always growing. There are likely as many boulder problems as rope routes. Recent visits by top climbers such as Chris Sharma, Fred Nicole and Jason Kehl have resulted in some truly incredible problems in the "harder than most humans can climb" category, and will certainly establish Arkansas as one of the premier bouldering destinations.

Please feel free to responsibly clean any unclimbed boulders or problems and establish as many new problems or variations as you desire.

Contact Information

Horseshoe Canyon Guest Ranch
HC 70, Box 261
Jasper, Arkansas 72641
800-480-9635 for reservations
870-446-2555 for climbing information
www.horseshoecanyon.com
www.climbhcr.com

Please send comments or new route and boulder problem information to:

Tom Hancock: tom@bostonmountainpress.com

Emergency Numbers

In the unfortunate event of an accident or emergency, please notify ranch personnel immediately so that they may assist in obtaining help.

Newton County Sheriff's Department
Jasper, Arkansas
870-446-5124

National Forest Department
Jasper, Arkansas
870-446-2228

North Arkansas Regional Medical Center
Harrison, Arkansas
870-365-2000

Tom Hancock on The Catholic Boat

CRACKHOUSE ALLEY

Crackhouse Alley was named and discovered by Christopher Columbus while he spread pestilence and disease across our... Actually it is not known who first discovered the climbing potential here, but we are going to give the credit to Alf Carter. Longtime local and climbing pioneer, Alf set the bar for the rest to follow. Many of the more difficult cracks were likely first climbed by Craig Thomas and Billy Bisswanger. Other local pioneers, such as T. Morris, the notorious Anderson brothers, Kerry Allen, Rich McDade, Mike Wintroath, and Willy Nelson, also left their marks on these cliffs. When Lick Hollow became the Ranch it is today, the cracks in the **Alley** and the **Confederate Cracks** were the only established routes on the property. The next step was to put up as many cherry sport lines as we could. Now the **Alley** is both a great sport and trad destination, which is climbable year-round.

To find this area, take the west bench road/trail above the cabins south and then right up a steep section to the top. Continue left at the sign on a footpath, over the mud hole and to the fence.

1. Hickadelic Jazzgrass 5.8 PG ★★
This route is literally above the west fence. Start this arête with some strenuous moves and continue on easy ground. (5 bolts) 60 ft.
FA: Jason Roy '02

2. Barley & Hops 5.8+ ★★
Just left of **420**, start in a thin dihedral up to a bulge. Pull over the bulge onto a slab face and climb to the top. (trad w/o anchors) 60 ft.
FA: Unknown

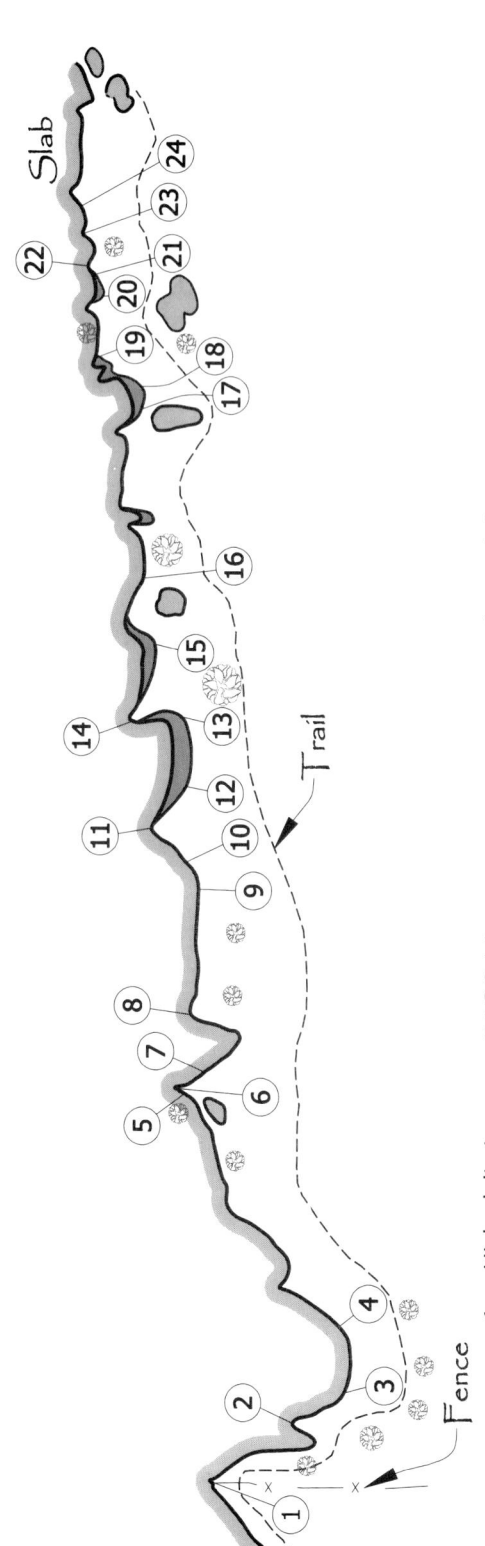

1. Hickadelic Jazzgrass 5.8 PG ★★
2. Barley & Hops 5.8+ ★★
3. 420 5.12a/b ★★★
4. Elephant Ear 5.11d ★★★
5. Captain Disco 5.10c ★★
6. Dirty Crack Whore 5.8 ★★
7. Hasenpfeffer 5.10b ★★★★
8. The Vegetable 5.8 PG
9. Milquetoast 5.11a ★★
10. Meatcake 5.10d ★★★
11. Old School 5.8+ ★
12. White Trash Took My Heavy Metal 5.12c ★★★
13. Electroglide 5.11b ★★★
14. The Catholic Boat 5.9+ ★★★
15. Introrectogestion 5.12b/c ★★★
16. Strong Men Also Cry 5.12b ★★
17. U235 5.13?
18. The Gigolo 5.12b ★★★★
19. T-Rex 5.10d ★★★★
20. Classique 5.11a ★★★★
21. Tsunami 5.12c ★★
22. Mortar Fire 5.9+ ★★
23. Hand Grenade 5.9+ ★
24. Wave 5.12b ★★

Crackhouse Alley

16 • *Crackhouse Alley*

3. **420 5.12a/b** ✶✶✶
Start on slab crimps to pockets. Continue up 5.9ish pockets in the overhang to a jug at the break. Pull out onto the second bulge and the boulder problem crux. 5.8 climbing takes you to the top. (7 bolts) 65 ft.
FA: Chad Watkins '02

4. **Elephant Ear 5.11d** ✶✶✶
Start just right of **420** on the same slab. Climb up and right to a jug and a good stance. From here, negotiate a sequential series of pockets to gain the easy climbing above. (7 bolts) 65 ft.
FA: Chad Watkins '02

5. **Captain Disco 5.10c** ✶✶
This route is thirty feet right of **Elephant Ear** and starts off a boulder/bench. Start stemming the wide crack. At the second bolt, pull onto the face/arête on small holds and negotiate a path up and right to jugs. Parallel the crack up brilliant orange rock to a small roof. Warning: The free-standing pillar is DANGEROUS. Pull the roof on good holds and continue to the top. (8 bolts) 60 ft.
FA: Chad Watkins '02

6. **Dirty Crack Whore 5.8** ✶✶
This is the nice, dirty, and wide crack to the right of **Captain Disco**. (trad, shares anchors) 60 ft.
FA: Alf Carter

7. **Hasenpfeffer 5.10b** ✶✶✶✶
This is a fun slab with great movement; it was originally done trad with three pieces! (9 bolts) 65 ft.
FA: Chad Watkins '02

8. **The Vegetable 5.8 PG**
Either start on **Hasenpfeffer** and move to the crack, or do the overhanging start. (trad w/o anchors) 65 ft.
FA: Unknown

9. **Milquetoast 5.11a** ✶✶
Start in a sort of scoop and move up left. Continue on easy ground to steeper rock. Move up and left through a steep section to the anchors. (9 bolts) 65 ft.
FA: Kerry Allen '02

10. **Meatcake 5.10d** ✶✶✶
Start on a small slab and climb up to the steep face. Climb out onto a difficult pocketed section ending on a jug to the left. Pull over onto the face and move right to the arête. Climb easy jugs to the top. (9 bolts) 65 ft.
FA: Chad Watkins '02

11. **Old School 5.8+** ✶
Climb the vegetated wide crack. (trad w/o anchors) 65ft.
FA: Unknown

12. **White Trash Took My Heavy Metal 5.12c** ✶✶✶
Beautiful stone and difficult moves lead to a crux at the roof. (5 bolts) 45 ft.
FA: Chad Watkins '04

13. **Electroglide 5.11b** ✶✶✶
Stick-clip the first bolt, and climb to the roof. Place a hand-sized piece at the roof, and fling yourself over the expanse to escape to the safety of the upper slab bolts. Don't forget to leave a long sling under the roof. (mixed w/6 bolts, anchors) 70 ft.
FA: Chris Lennox '01

14. The Catholic Boat 5.9+ ★★★
This is a great crack with two starts. Choose either start and climb to the upper dihedral with good hand and fist climbing to the top. (trad w/o anchors) 70 ft.
FA: Unknown

15. Introrectogestion 5.12b/c ★★★
This route is not as hard as eating with your rectum, but it is formidable. Climb the slab to the hanging arête and move out onto the arête and up to the roof. Pull past the roof to a steep headwall. Continue to the top on thin holds. (9 bolts) 70 ft.
FA: Chad Watkins '04

16. Strong Men Also Cry 5.12b ★★
Walk to the right of **Introrectogestion** about forty feet and behind the block. Start on the slab and move up left to a small roof. Pull the roof and move left again to anchors. (7 bolts) 55 ft.
FA: Kerry Allen '02

17. U235 5.13?
This route remains a project; if anyone has done this route, please let us know. Start at the overhang and climb into a shallow dihedral. Continue up the dihedral to a bulge. Pull a couple of freakishly hard moves and you gain the anchors. (9 bolts) 60 ft.
FA: ?

18. The Gigolo 5.12b ★★★★
Start at an overhang and climb into a shallow dihedral. There is a long pocket move above the dihedral that will be difficult for shorter climbers. Good technical climbing leads to a bulge. Pull through sloper-crimps and a cryptic crux to reach the anchors. (9 bolts) 65 ft.
FA: Rich McDade '02

19. T-Rex 5.10d ★★★★
Start this route with some chimney moves and then move left onto the ramp. Continue on easy ground to steeper rock. Climb up overhanging stone for a long move to a good jug. Pull out right and then back left, and hoist yourself up to escape the roof. Then make two more moves to the anchors. (7 bolts) 60 ft.
FA: Chad Watkins '03

20. Classique (a.k.a. The Anderson Brothers Strike Again) 5.11a ★★★★
Climb the dihedral finger crack to a roof. Traverse left (crux) and continue up the sustained 5.9 flake. There is some debate over who first did this route, but all that is really important is that everyone climbs it! (trad w/anchors) 60 ft.
FA: Unknown

21. Tsunami 5.12c ★★
Start in the scoop dihedral just right of **Classique** and move out right to the arête. Climb to the lip and make a difficult move onto a slab. From here, simply climb the obvious seam. (9 bolts) 60 ft.
FA: Chad Watkins '02

22. Mortar Fire 5.9+ ★★
This hands to fingers crack is a little vegetated. (mixed w/1 bolt, no anchors) 60 ft.
FA: Unknown

23. Hand Grenade 5.9+ ★
Climb the hand and fist crack. (trad w/o anchors) 60 ft.
FA: Unknown

Nathan Lindstrom on Meatcake

24. Wave 5.12b ✶✶
Start in a dihedral and climb up and left onto a slab. Move through two bulges on very thin moves, then out right to an arête, and some tricky moves at the end. (11 bolts) 60 ft.
FA: Unknown

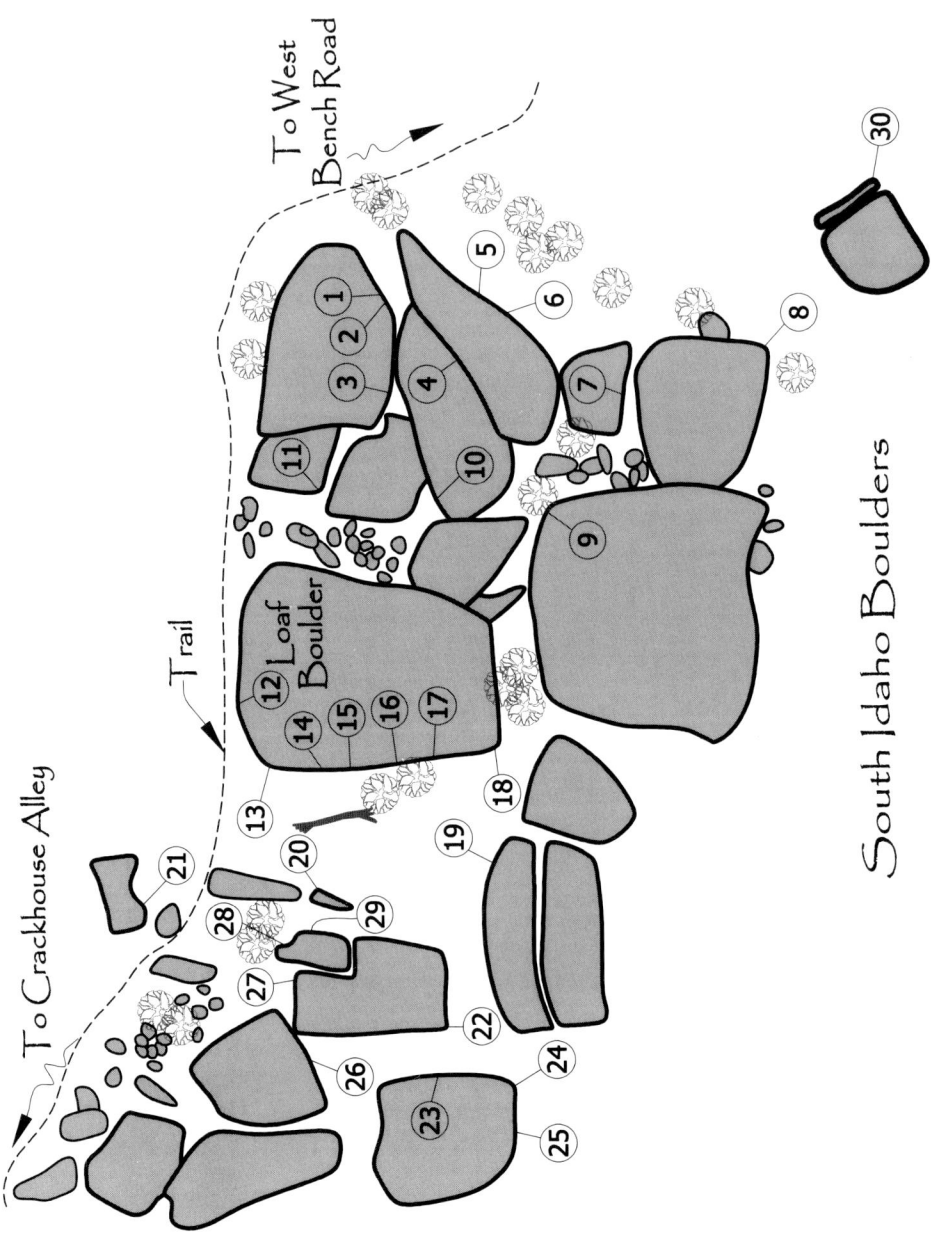

The South Idaho Boulders lie on the south side of the trail to **Crackhouse Alley** just below the route **W.M.A.** The area contains some of the most coveted sends on the Ranch, including the mega classic **Dig Dug** and the featureless **Glass Bowl**.

1. **French Bread V4** - Sloper arête.
2. **Chicken of the Sea V6** - Start on the left side of the sloping arête, and top-out left on slopers.
3. **The Rib V7** - Start on crimps on face and go left on perfect ledge.
4. **Glass Bowl V10** - SDS on sloper and crimp and straight up to top on crimps.
5. **Dark Elf V10** - SDS on right arête. Climb up and to the left through opening.
6. **Thought Police V4** - Climb slab on pockets to sloper.
7. **Double Standard V3** - SDS, climb face.
8. **Numerical Methods V8** - SDS on undercling and up arête.
9. **California Daydream V5** - Climb arête.
10. **Just Sad V2** - Climb to top on slopers.
11. **The Edge V6** - SDS on crimpers and top-out over lip.
12. **Jekyll V1** - Slab
13. **Bottoms Up V2** - Climb pockets to sloper.
14. **Dig Dug V4** - SDS under roof, climb out roof and up to sloper top-out.
15. **Fraziac V5** - SDS to right of **Dig Dug** under roof, to crimp under roof and trend left to **Dig Dug** finish.
16. **Tree Left V5** - SDS under roof and top-out left of tree.
17. **Tree Right V3** - Same start as **Tree Left** but trend right of tree and top-out.
18. **Quite Time V1** - SDS on jugs.
19. **Fontastic V6** - Pocket start, then move left and up to sloper top-out.
20. **Rainshadow V1** - Arête.
21. **The Flat V3** - Start on left side of lip and traverse right on lip.
22. **Ruthless Arête V11** - SDS right of arête on good ledge, climb left to arête and flip onto adjoining face of arête. Climb to top. Stand start on second face to top-out is V9.
23. **Quagmire V2** - SDS on crimps, then straight up to top out finish.
24. **Golden Palomino V9** - Start on high crimps to left and right of arête, fire up to ledge, then climb up and left on arête.
25. **Legends of the Fall V8** - Start on face crimps, then large deadpoint to slopey crimp, and trend left to rounded arête finish.
26. **The Crescent V3** - Start down and left of crescent hold on slopers, climb up slab to crescent, and continue to lip. At lip, trend right to top-out.
27. **War Bonnet V4** - SDS under roof and top-out on vertical face.
28. **Dirty Bitch V3** - Start on crimp and slope to sloper top-out.
29. **Even Dirtier V5** - SDS under roof on pinch and crimp. Trend right to **Dirty Bitch** top-out.
30. **Razor's Edge V7** - SDS on crimps, climb arête.

South Idaho Boulders • 21

Amanda Smith on the ever so sweet W.M.A.

Confederate Cracks

The Confederate Cracks hold the bulk of classic cracks on the Ranch, from the gnarly underclings of **I Fought Piranhas**, to the cool smooth pleasure of **Hackberry Crack**. You can test your mastery of the wide by wriggling your way up, **In The Crack or On Your Back**. Then try the thin hands crux of **W.M.A.** Whatever you choose, its sure to be a crowd-pleaser. If slab climbing is your game, then the **Black Slabs** area is a must. The routes there range from 5.8 to 5.12 and will satisfy any slab addict. Don't forget about the **Walls of Moria**. This area is cool for summer afternoons and warm for winter mornings.

To find this area, take the west bench road/trail above the cabins south and then right up a steep section to the top. Continue right at the sign on a footpath. The obvious large streaked slabs are the **Walls of Moria**.

1. **The Mud, The Blood & The Beer 5.11b** ✶✶✶
Once hidden by a large poison ivy vine, this enticing thin finger crack on the wall to the left of **Deft Jam** is a beautiful climb. If you climb this route, you owe the first ascensionist a beer for his heroic cleaning effort. (mixed w/2 bolts, anchors) 55 ft.
FA: John Sizemore '05

2. **Deft Jam 5.9+** ✶✶✶
You can find this obvious splitter hands to fists dihedral just uphill of the **South Idaho Boulders**. Start on a bench behind a boulder. At the top, traverse right to the **Door Prize** anchors. (trad w/anchors) 55 ft.
FA: Tony Morris

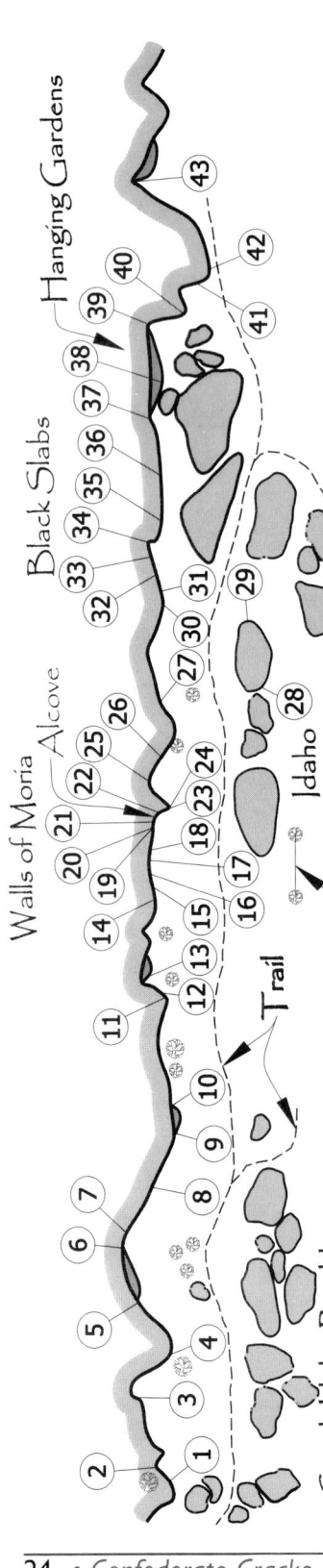

Confederate Cracks

1. The Mud, The Blood & The Beer 5.11b ★★★
2. Deft Jam 5.9+ ★★★
3. Door Prize 5.12a ★★
4. Mountain Meadow Massacre 5.11b/c PG ★
5. Fat Bastard 5.10d ★★
6. I Fought Piranhas 5.11c ★★★
7. I Fought Guppies 5.9 ★
8. W.M.A. 5.9+ ★★★★
9. Up Your Buttress 5.10a ★★★★
10. Public Access 5.7
11. Chinese Soul Food 5.11b ★★★
12. Roary Breaker 5.13a ★★
13. Mad Man with an Afro 5.10c ★
14. Stove Top 5.10a ★★★
15. Devil's Candy 5.10d ★★★
16. Gimp and Wheezer 5.10a ★★★★
17. Tales of Ribaldry 5.8 ★
18. Fighting Uruk-hai 5.11b ★★★
19. Frogger 5.11d ★★★
20. Stem Cell Research 5.9+ ★
21. Left Hook of God 5.9- ★ PG
22. Right Hook of Allah 5.8 ★ PG
23. Balrog 5.11c ★
24. Solid 5.9+ ★★★★
25. Entwash 5.9+ ★
26. Treebeard 5.8- ★★★
27. Hackberry Crack 5.9- ★★★★★
28. Message to Hairy Back Man 5.10a ★★
29. Unnamed 5.10d ★★
30. Toxic Dementia 5.12b ★★★
31. Knob Creek 5.10c ★★★★
32. Newton's Law 5.11c ★★★
33. Tiny Bubbles 5.12b ★★
34. Shelob's Lair 5.10a PG
35. The Seamstress 5.10a ★★★
36. Product of Kush 5.8 ★★
37. Gilgamek Vagina 5.9 ★★
38. Nova Monkey 5.12b ★★★★
39. The Wet One 5.9+ PG
40. XXX 5.12d ★★
41. Sissy-made Training Academy 5.12b ★
42. Up Yours Ashcroft 5.7 ★
43. In The Crack or On Your Back 5.10d ★★★★

3. **Door Prize 5.12a** ✶✶
This striking, steep arête is good for testing shoes. (8 bolts) 55 ft.
FA: Justin Fiola '04

4. **Mountain Meadow Massacre 5.11b/c PG** ✶
This route is just down the hill and to the right of **Door Prize**, to the right of the big tree. Climb the finger crack to the right-facing flake, then move right to the face/arête. (mixed w/2 bolts, anchors) 65 ft.
FA: Rich McDade '01

5. **Fat Bastard 5.10d** ✶✶
Down right around the corner from **Mountain Meadow Massacre** is a detached flake/off-width leading up to a small roof. Move left out of the roof up to the slab headwall and onto the hanging arête. Mount the arête on the right and continue to the anchors. (9 bolts) 70 ft.
FA: Chad Watkins '02

6. **I Fought Piranhas 5.11c** ✶✶✶
Move uphill right of **Fat Bastard** to find this innocent, overhanging, right-leaning off-width crack in the corner. (trad w/anchors) 50 ft.
FA: Kerry Allen '01

7. **I Fought Guppies 5.9** ✶
This is the short off-width just right of **I Fought Piranhas**. (trad w/o anchors) 50 ft.
FA: Kerry Allen '01

8. **W.M.A. 5.9+** ✶✶✶✶
A splitter hand/fist crack leads to a thin hands crux. If you can't find this superb crack, just look for the deforestation. (trad w/anchors) 60 ft.
FA: McCree Anderson

9. **Up Your Buttress 5.10a** ✶✶✶
Just downhill and to the right of **W.M.A.** on the left side of the pillar, start either on the block or in the chimney. Enjoy excellent, sustained climbing up this awesome crack. (trad w/anchors) 70 ft.
FA: Eric Hudkins 01'

10. **Public Access 5.7**
Climb the off-width chimney located on the right side of the pillar. (trad w/o anchors) 65 ft.
FA: Unknown

11. **Chinese Soul Food 5.11b** ✶✶✶
Powerful moves up a slightly overhanging, pocketed arête lead to easier climbing followed by a few more steep moves to the anchors. (11 bolts) 70 ft.
FA: Chad Watkins '02

12. **Roary Breaker 5.13a** ✶✶
Climb the difficult, thin face variation to the right of **Chinese Soul Food**. (10 bolts) 65 ft.
FA: Rich McDade '03

13. **Mad Man with an Afro 5.10c** ✶
This is the technical face climb with a boulder problem crux on black rock just right of the dihedral. (5 bolts) 50 ft.
FA: Jason Roy '02

14. Stove Top 5.10a ✶✶✶
This is the first slab route on the left end of the **Walls of Moria**. An easy start leads to a difficult slab above. (9 bolts) 60 ft.
FA: Kerry Allen '02

15. Devil's Candy 5.10d ✶✶✶
Just right of **Stove Top**, pull off the ground on small holds up to slopers and pockets and up to the technical slab. (11 bolts) 65 ft.
FA: Chad Watkins '02

16. Gimp and Wheezer 5.10a ✶✶✶✶
This route has excellent climbing and is less technical than **Devil's Candy**. Start on pockets just left of the wide crack and climb through difficult moves to the slab headwall and a large water groove. (11 bolts) 65 ft.
FA: Chad Watkins '02

17. Tales of Ribaldry 5.8 ✶
Climb the obvious off-width slab. (trad w/o anchors) 65 ft.
FA: Alf Carter

18. Fighting Uruk-hai 5.11b ✶✶✶
A boulder problem start leads to technical slab climbing up a beautiful black streak. This route is located at the far right side of the **Walls of Moria**. (7 bolts) 60 ft.
FA: Chad Watkins '02

19. Frogger 5.11d ✶✶✶
Climb up on the bench on the right end of the **Walls of Moria** and climb the striking, overhanging fin/arête. You'll understand the name after doing this route. (6 bolts) 50 ft.
FA: Chad Watkins '02

20. Stem Cell Research 5.9+ ✶
Stem and bridge your way up the **Frogger** bolt line. (6 bolts) 50 ft.
FA: Clay Frisbie '02

21. Left Hook of God 5.9- ✶ PG
Climb the left chimney crack to a roof, then traverse left to the **Frogger** anchors. (trad, shares anchors) 50 ft.
FA: Kerry Allen '02

22. Right Hook of Allah 5.8 ✶ PG
Climb the wide crack to the right of **Left Hook of God** to the roof, then out the roof to the hanging dihedral. (trad, shares anchors) 50 ft.
FA: Kerry Allen '02

23. Balrog 5.11c ✶✶
This is the technical face straight up the black water groove and arête. Move right onto the face and continue up steep climbing to a slab finish. (8 bolts) 55 ft.
FA: Jason Roy '02

24. Solid 5.9+ ✶✶✶
A difficult start on the arête with delicate moves leads to easier but slightly pumpy climbing above and to the left of the arête. (7 bolts) 60 ft.
FA: Kerry Allen '02

25. Entwash 5.9+ ✶
In the corner just up the hill right of **Solid**, climb the thin, ever-widening crack to the anchors. (trad w/anchors) 55 ft.
FA: Chad Watkins '03

Amanda Smith awash on Knob Creek — Photo: Chad Watkins

26. Treebeard 5.8- ★★★
Climb the obvious hand to fist crack just down and right of the **Entwash** dihedral. This route features excellent climbing on good gear. (trad w/anchors) 50 ft.
FA: Unknown

27. Hackberry Crack 5.9- ★★★★★
This is the best crack on the ranch! When you climb this one you will giggle. Enjoy great jams with good hand to fist-sized gear. (trad w/anchors) 50 ft.
FA: Unknown

28. Message to Hairy Back Man 5.10a ★★
This fun climb is located in the **Idaho Boulders** on the southern side of the large boulder below **Hackberry Crack** in the. (5 bolts) 50 ft.
FA: Jason Roy '02

29. Unnamed 5.10d ★★
Located on the northern side of the aforementioned boulder, this climb is quite a bit harder than it's neighbor, **Message to Hairy Back Man**. (5 bolts) 50 ft.
FA: Tony Morris

30. Toxic Dementia 5.12b ★★★
This route marks the left end of the **Black Slabs** area and features technical arête climbing with some difficult moves. (9 bolts) 60 ft.
FA: Mike Wintroath '02

31. Knob Creek 5.10c ★★★★
About thirty feet right of **Toxic Dementia**, start on a slab with black knobs and continue up and slightly left on more knobs and slopers to an exciting finish. (7 bolts) 50 ft.
FA: Chad Watkins '02

32. Newton's Law 5.11c ★★★
This sweet slab starts off easy but becomes more powerful and technical until reaching a small roof. Crank through the roof to gain the anchors. (7 bolts) 55 ft.
FA: Chad Watkins '02

33. Tiny Bubbles 5.12b ★★
Just right of **Newton's Law**, move up to a large loaf-block. From here, climb slightly left through difficult slab moves to a small roof. Pull the roof and continue to the **Newton's Law** anchors. (7 bolts) 55 ft.
FA: Chad Watkins '02

34. Shelob's Lair 5.10a PG
Wedge yourself in and wriggle your way to the top of this obvious chimney. (trad w/o anchors) 50 ft.
FA: Dave McGee '01

35. The Seamstress 5.10a ★★★
Located just right of **Shelob's Lair**, a tough start leads to a thin seam. Continue in the seam until you reach a horizontal break with a small stump, which may be looped with a long sling to calm the nerves. Climb into the dihedral and pull over a small bulge to reach the anchors. (5 bolts) 50 ft.
FA: Tom Hancock '02

36. Product of Kush 5.8 ★★
Start this one twenty feet right of **The Seamstress**. Climb the serpentine seam up and right. (4 bolts) 45 ft.
FA: Jason Roy '02

37. Gilgamek Vagina 5.9 ★★
Walk down into the **Hanging Gardens** to find the start of this route. Climb the huge crack that diminishes at the roof. Move up and left at the roof to find the anchors. (trad w/anchors) 50 ft.
FA: Chad Watkins '02

38. Nova Monkey 5.12b ★★★★
Start on the right edge of the **Gilgamek Vagina** and move right onto the face. Climb up to the roof. Difficult moves out the roof past fixed draws will get you to the jugs at the anchors of this excellent climb. (9 bolts) 60 ft.
FA: Chad Watkins '02

39. The Wet One 5.9+ PG
This dihedral is always wet. If you climb it, you should give yourself a beer. (trad w/anchors) 60 ft.
FA: Unknown

40. XXX 5.12d ★
This striking arête is marred only by the boulders stacked against it. A tough, bouldery start will get you to the upper arête. Climb delicate moves to the top. (7 bolts)
FA: Unknown

41. Sissy-made Training Academy 5.12b ★
From **XXX**, walk through the portal to the north and make a right at the next corner. **Sissy-made** is just to the right of this corner. Start on thin, balancy moves and continue on more thin moves to jugs. Move through the crux to the right and then back left and on to the anchors. (7 bolts) 50 ft.
FA: Chad Watkins '02

42. Up Yours Ashcroft 5.7 ★
Start on the blocks down and right of **Sissy-made Training Academy** and climb the arête to the cold shuts. (trad w/anchors) 50 ft.
FA: Tony Morris

43. In The Crack or On Your Back 5.10d ★★★★
This will be your off-width exam for the day! Bring #4 Camalots and a #5 Camalot for the crux. There is nothing fancy about this climb; you need only to go up... if you can. (trad w/o anchors) 50 ft.
FA: Unknown

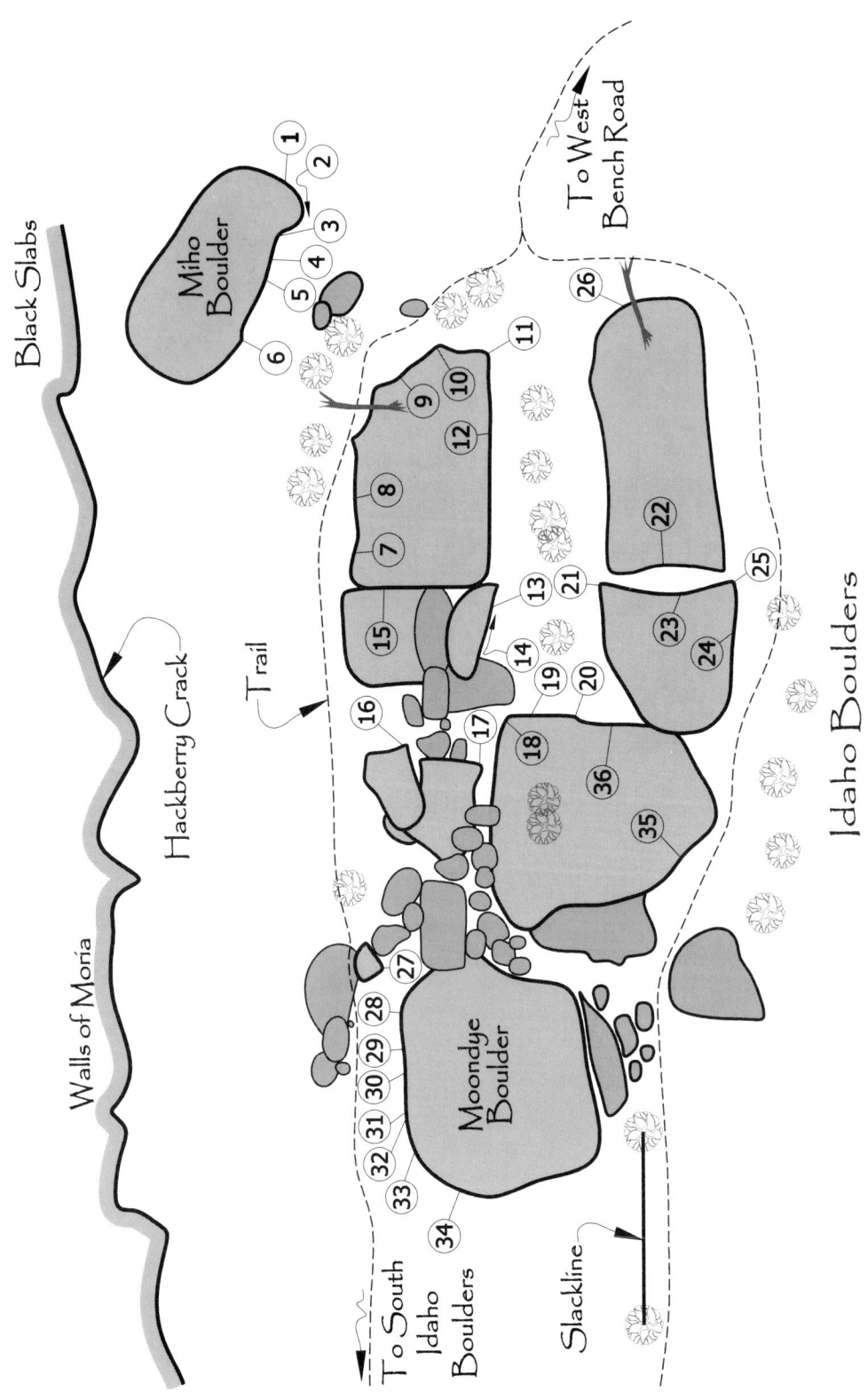

The Idaho Boulders are found below the **Black Slabs** area of the **Confederate Cracks**. They can be reached from the north via the west bench road/trail. The **Idaho Boulders** were one of the original boulderfields to be developed, and they offer a wide range of fine problems. Don't miss out on the classic **Momento** and if you are feeling burly, **Moondye** is an incredible testpiece.

1. **South Bound V3** - SDS on sloper, straight up to jugs.
2. **Alabama Ahead V4** - SDS on sloper, traverse left on sloper-lip and finish on **Udaho**.
3. **Udaho V3** - SDS on underclings, mantle on huge sloper.
4. **Miho V7** - SDS on lieback crack to a gaston, trend left to top-out with tooth.
5. **Hot Tub Ho V6** - Link up and **Udaho** and **Miho**.
5. **Miho's Cousin V8** - SDS on jugs, throw to mono, top-out with tooth.
6. **Project V?** - Climb dihedral.
7. **Unnamed V1**
8. **Unnamed V1**
9. **High Five V4** - Dyno from crimps.
10. **Momento V5** - Arête left of **High Five**.
11. **Old English V3** - Slopey and highball arête.
12. **Puddle Project V?** - Highball slab.
13. **Swad V4** - Match on crimp, top-out on slopers.
14. **Cold Sore V4** - Lip traverse left to right and top-out on **Swad**.
15. **Unnamed V1** - Slab
16. **Make You Cuss V4** - Climb sharp arête to jugs.
17. **Project V?** - Arête
18. **Dan's Arete V2** - Climb arête.
19. **Project V?**
20. **Project V?**
21. **Mount and Up V6** - SDS, climb arête.
22. **Scott's Slab V0** - Slab in middle of wall.
23. **Isolation V8** - Start matched on left sloper, go out right to ledge, and top-out.
24. **Unnamed V1** - SDS in hueco and top-out.
25. **Get Started V5** - SDS on arête and climb up and left to finish.
26. **Dave's Problem V4** - SDS to runnel top-out.
27. **Dan's Arete V2** - Shelf top-out.
28. **Ferris Wheel V2** - Steep arête, short.
29. **Heaven in a Can V4** - Left on crimp, right on sloper.
30. **Moondye V9** - SDS on rail and sloper, go to sloping edges and dyno to top.
   Moondye Stand Start V4 - Start on last three moves of SDS version
31. **Cloud of Stars V7** - Start on jugs, go to flake, and sloping block.
32. **Kung Fu V8** - Start on jug, traverse left and finish on **Moondye**.
33. **Chuck Wagon V6** - Dyno for the jug just to the right of **Cloud of Stars**.
34. **Frightened and Horny V0** - Highball slab.
35. **Message to Hairy Back Man 5.10a** - Sport climb
36. **Unnamed 5.10d** - Sport climb

Idaho Boulders • 31

Frank Niles proves that you don't need large muscles to climb Crockostimpy

Ren & Stimpy Wall

The **Ren & Stimpy** area offers a small collection of short, bouldery routes that overhang nicely. It's hard to pick out the best one because they all have fantastic moves. So if you are looking for good powerful routes, this area is highly recommended. It is a good summer area because it stays shaded most of the day. For winter climbing, it gets pretty cold, but that's also when the friction is best.

To find this area, take the same path as you would for the **Prophecy Wall** but at the top of the trail go left instead of right. Walk fifty yards and the trail will be on your right, marked by a sign on a tree.

1. **The Big Sleep 5.12b** ✭✭✭
Start on the left side of the shallow cave and climb the steep arête. (4 bolts) 45 ft.
FA: Chad Watkins '03

2. **Crockostimpy 5.12d** ✭✭✭✭
Start in the center of the overhang and move up and right on jugs and thin holds to a break, then back left. Climb over a bulge, trending right on thin holds to a tough clip at the third bolt. Negotiate two cruxes to gain the jug at the end of the bulge and easier climbing to the anchors. (5 bolts) 50 ft.
FA: Chad Watkins '03

3. **Space Madness 5.11d/12a** ✭✭✭
Twenty feet right of **Crockostimpy**, start in a shallow dihedral up to a small roof. Move just right of the roof, then back to the sharp arête. Continue up strenuous moves to jugs and climb to the top. (4 bolts) 50 ft.
FA: Chad Watkins '03

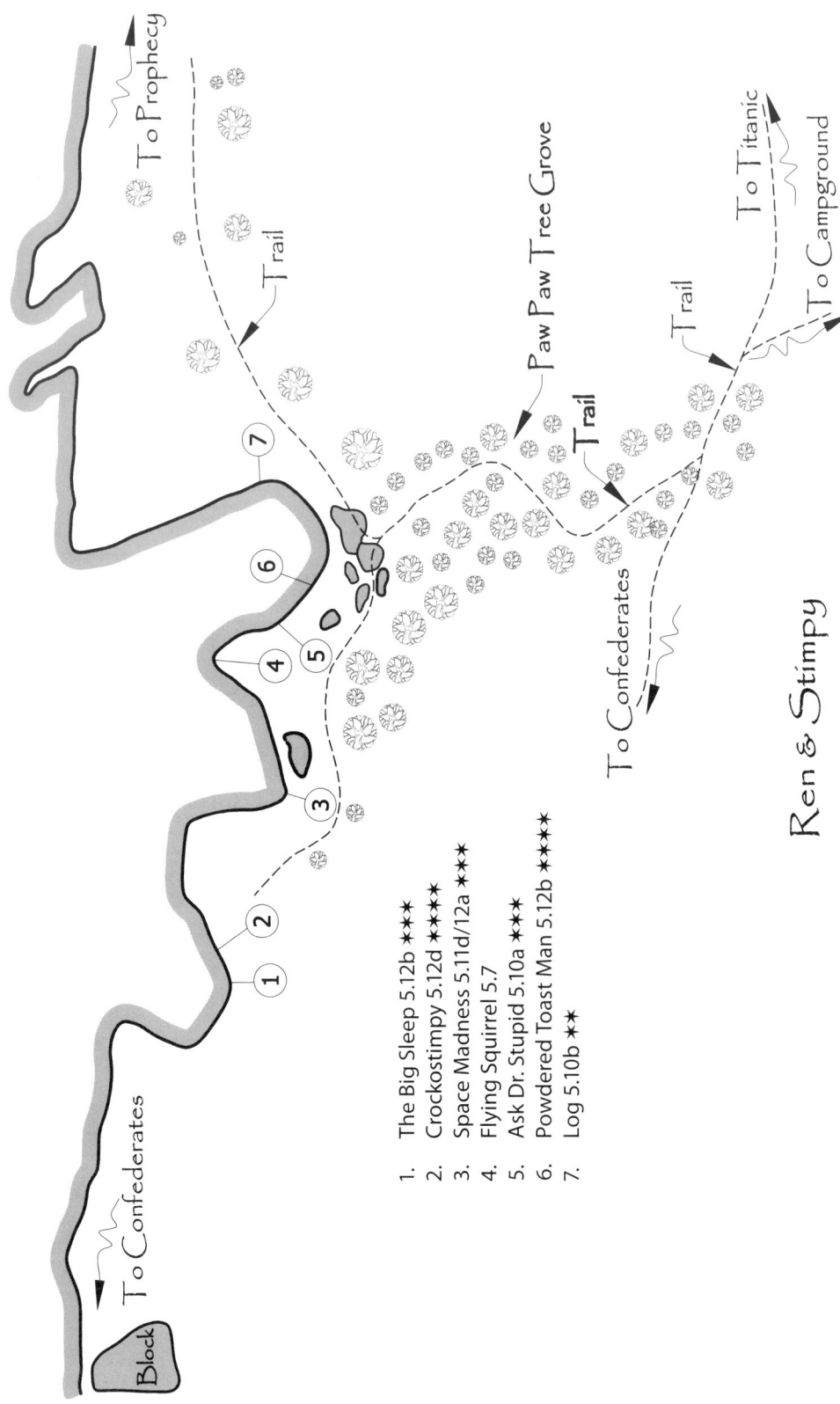

Sean Cook sets up for The Big Sleep

4. Flying Squirrel 5.7
This is the dihedral crack to the right of **Space Madness**. (trad w/o anchors) 50 ft.
FA: Unknown

5. Ask Dr. Stupid 5.10a ★★★
Just right of the dihedral, start on small holds. Move up and slightly left to gain the roof. Pull up and right over the small part of the roof and continue to the top on good holds. (5 bolts) 50 ft.
FA: Jason Roy '03

6. Powdered Toast Man 5.12b ★★★★
Start under the large roof on slab moves. Climb out the roof on flakes to a jug. From the jug, make a long move to a decent hold, and then reach left to a crimp-rail. A long move through the crux leads to jugs and the anchors. (4 bolts) 45 ft.
FA: Chad Watkins '03

7. Log 5.10b ★★
Around the corner to the right of **Powdered Toast Man**, start on overhanging moves to gain the vertical climbing above. Tricky climbing guards the anchors. (4 bolts) 45 ft.
FA: Chad Watkins '03

Chad Watkins on The Prophet

PROPHECY WALL

The **Prophecy Wall** is a striking piece of stone capped by a six-foot roof. Routes on this wall range from easy jug-hauls to crimpy power-fests. The hardest of these is **The Prophet**, which stood for three years without being climbed until 2005 when Chris Sharma sent the route on his fourth try. You don't have to be superhuman to climb here though. Try your luck on **Learning To Fly** and if that goes well you may be ready for the incredibly fun roof of **Taliban Soup**. This area is good on warm days but tends to sweat when it is humid. Winter is also good if you can stay warm.

To find this area, hike north from the teepee on the campground road up the steep hill going west. At the bench, take the steep road/trail directly in front of you to the west bench road/trail. Head south on the trail to a footpath that leads up to the cliffs. At the top of the trailhead back to the north and you will see the wall on your left.

1. **The Prophet 5.13d/14a** ★★★★
Thin, bouldery moves lead to the roof, and then left onto the sloper and the sidepull. Mantle onto the upper face and stab for a small hold four feet up. Continue on good holds to anchors. (7 bolts) 50 ft.
FA: Chris Sharma '05

2. **Granny Tranny 5.12a** ★★
This route starts fifteen feet right of **The Prophet** and shares the start of **Taliban Soup**. After the first move, climb left on small holds, then up to larger ones. Balancy moves put you under the roof. Climb out right at the roof to the anchors. (7 bolts) 60 ft.
FA: Kerry Allen '02

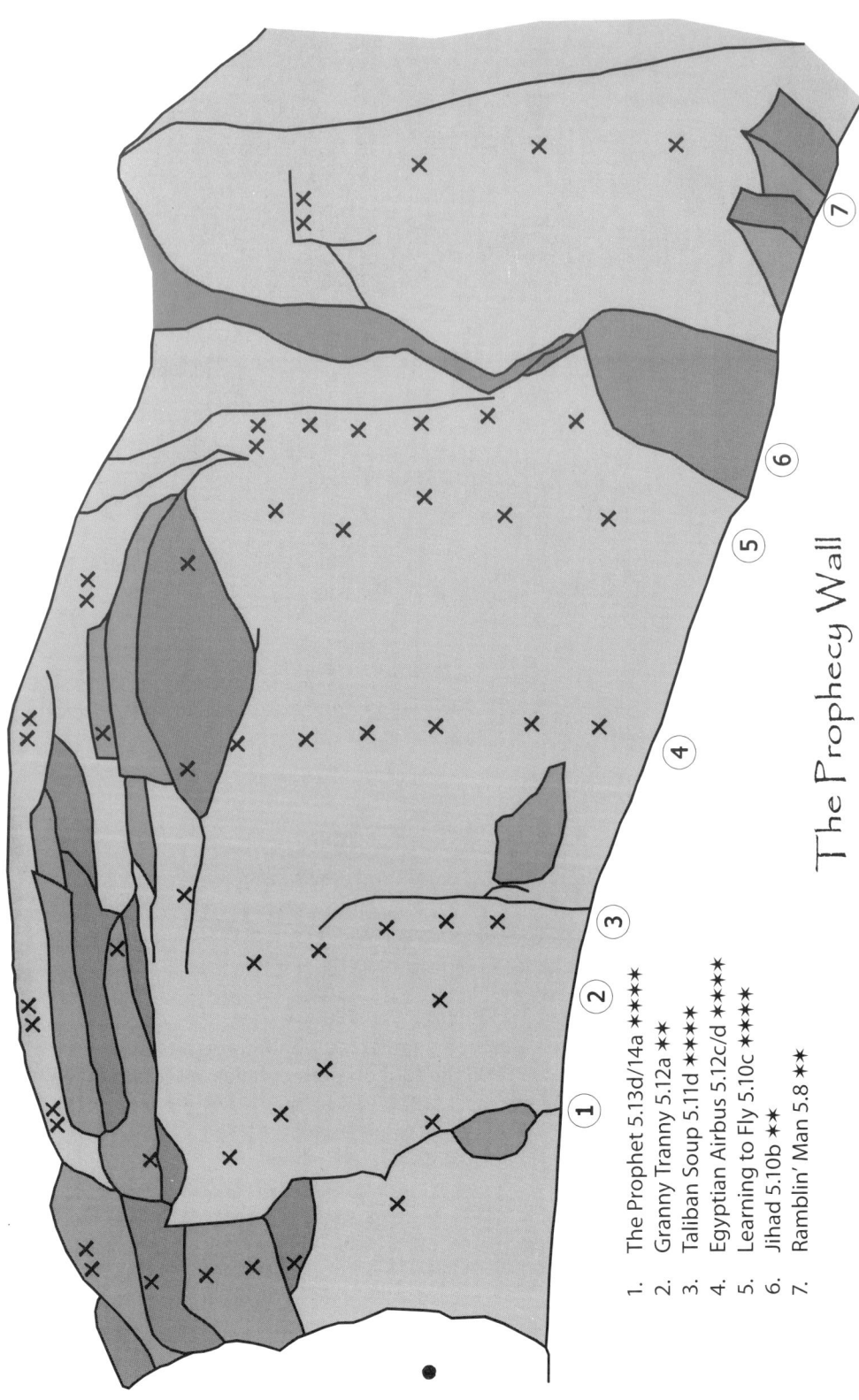

Chris Robertson floats up Taliban Soup

3. Taliban Soup 5.11d **

Climb the steep slab straight up to the triangular block. Move left up to the roof clipping fixed draws then climb straight out the roof on huge plates. (8 bolts/4 fixed) 65 ft.

FA: Chad Watkins '02

4. Egyptian Airbus 5.12c/d **

Start seven feet right of **Taliban Soup** on big holds to a stance. Thin moves up the bulge gain another stance. Continue up the slab to the right side of a triangular block under the roof. From here, step right, clipping fixed draws, to small holds and a long move up to a large block. Traverse left to a pod. From the pod, set up left on small holds to make the four-foot lunge out right to a large hold. Continue out the roof to anchors. (9 bolts/4 fixed) 65 ft.

FA: Chad Watkins '04

5. Learning to Fly 5.10c **

Start five feet right of **Egyptian Airbus** on good holds. Continue up and slightly left towards the right edge of the roof. Pull the roof on perfect holds and climb to the anchors. This is a great route but beware of the wicked pump and the subsequent flying lesson! (7 bolts) 65 ft.

FA: Chris Lennox '02

6. Jihad 5.10b **

Start just right of **Learning to Fly** and move right to the first bolt. Climb the blunt arête on good holds. (5 bolts) 50 ft.

FA: Chad Watkins '03

7. Ramblin' Man 5.8 **

Start on the right side of the adjacent wall to the right of **Jihad**. Climb up and left to anchors two-thirds of the way up. (4 bolts) 45 ft.

FA: Chris Lennox '02

Chad Watkins struggles to the surface on Cradle of the Deep

The Titanic

The Titanic boulder is a popular place to climb simply because of its unique shape. This area is a must-see for the striking prow, **Cradle Of the Deep,** a seemingly impossible wafer-thin fin that extends from the north end of the boulder. But you don't have to be endowed with bulging forearms to climb here, as there are plenty of fun, moderate routes. The formation can be climbed year-round; just follow or avoid the sun.

To find this area, head west up the steep road from the **West Campground** to the west bench road/trail. From here, the formation will be obvious. Head south on the west bench road/trail past the formation to the first footpath heading back to the northwest. **The Titanic** can also be approached from north along the cliff line trail.

1. **Starboard List 5.11a** ★★★
On the downhill side of the block, start on the bench to climb this formidable crack. Hand to rattly finger-sized gear will protect this short but mean crack. (trad w/anchors) 30 ft.
FA: Unknown

2. **Cracked Rib 5.11a** ★★
This route is on the square southern end of the block. Scramble up to the first bolt, and be ready for some thin moves afterwards. Kerry had a broken rib when he climbed this route. (3 bolts) 30 ft.
FA: Kerry Allen '02

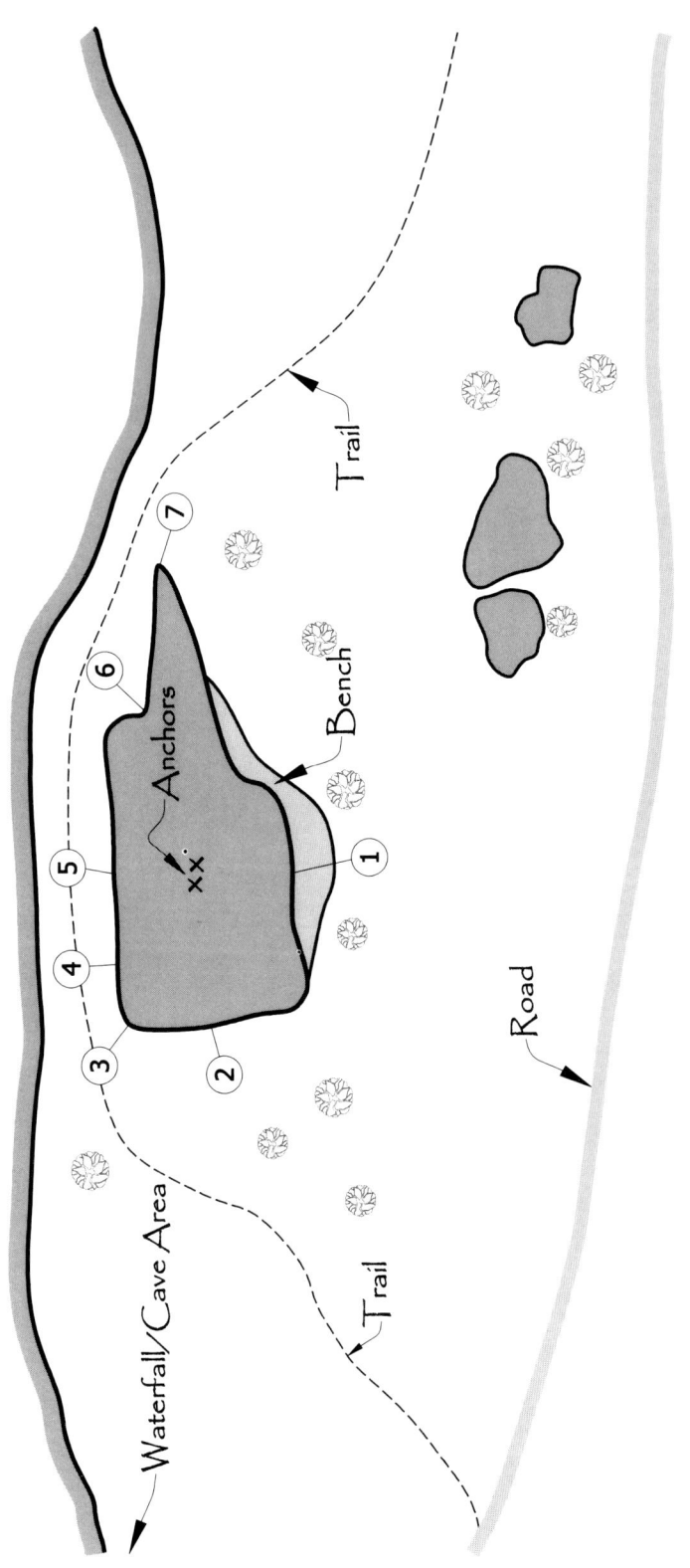

1. Starboard List 5.11a ★★★
2. Cracked Rib 5.11a ★★
3. Squirrel Deck 5.8+ ★★★
4. The Lookout 5.9+ ★★
5. Breach 5.9+ PG ★★
6. Port Side 5.10d ★★★★
7. Cradle of the Deep 5.13 ★★★★

The Titanic

Srin Surapanani cranking down on Starboard List

3. Squirrel Deck 5.8+ ✭✭✭
Climb the fun arête on the uphill southern end of the block. (4 bolts) 30 ft.
FA: Chad Watkins '02

4. The Lookout 5.9+ ✭✭
To the left of **Squirrel Deck**, climb straight up thin moves to larger holds and the anchors. (3 bolts) 30 ft.
FA: Chad Watkins '02

5. Breach 5.9+ PG ✭✭
This is the obvious splitter on the uphill side of the block. Climb crumbly holds to scary plates in the roof and an exciting top-out. This was the route to do on this block before the others were bolted. The roof protects well with a #3 or #4 Camalot. BEWARE OF LOOSE ROCK! (trad w/o anchors) 30 ft.
FA: Unknown

6. Port Side 5.10d ✭✭✭✭
Climb the smooth dihedral left of **Breach**. This quality route is thin, sustained, and stemmy. (5 bolts) 35 ft.
FA: Clay Frisbie '01

7. Cradle of the Deep 5.13 ✭✭✭✭
This is a truly classic climb and one of the most striking lines anywhere! To send this route you will have to muster every skill you have and plenty of power. A variation to the top-out can be done by heading out right onto the face past one bolt. (6 bolts) 35 ft.
FA: Nathaniel Walker '03

Jason Roy feasts on Crimp Scampi

the NORTH FORTY

The North Forty is by far the most popular and visited crag at the Ranch. The area offers a vast range of classic bolted sport climbs for all levels of climbers and can be climbed year-round.

Largely hidden from view, **The North Forty** was one of the last places on the Ranch to be explored and developed. Many of the routes were originally done either solo or on gear with minimal bolt protection. After much debate the climbs were eventually completely bolted. This metamorphosis turned marginally protected, seldom climbed routes into instant classics.

A few of the more classic lines include such routes as **Around the Fur,** a superb 5.8 line with unusual features. **Crimp Scampi** is by far the best 5.10 at **The North Forty** while **Sonny Jim** is a good challenge for the 5.11 climber. If you are feeling 5.13 strong, set your sights on **Venus Butterfly**. **The North Forty** is so well traveled that no "bushwhacking" is required. You might think twice on busy weekends though; it gets pretty crowded!

To find this area, hike north from the **West Campground** along the west bench road/trail up the steep hill to the bluff.

1. **Sour Girl 5.10a** ✷✷✷
This is the fun pocketed route with a cool roof on the north side of the large boulder located at the top of the steep road on the left. (4 bolts) 35 ft.
FA: Chad Watkins '02

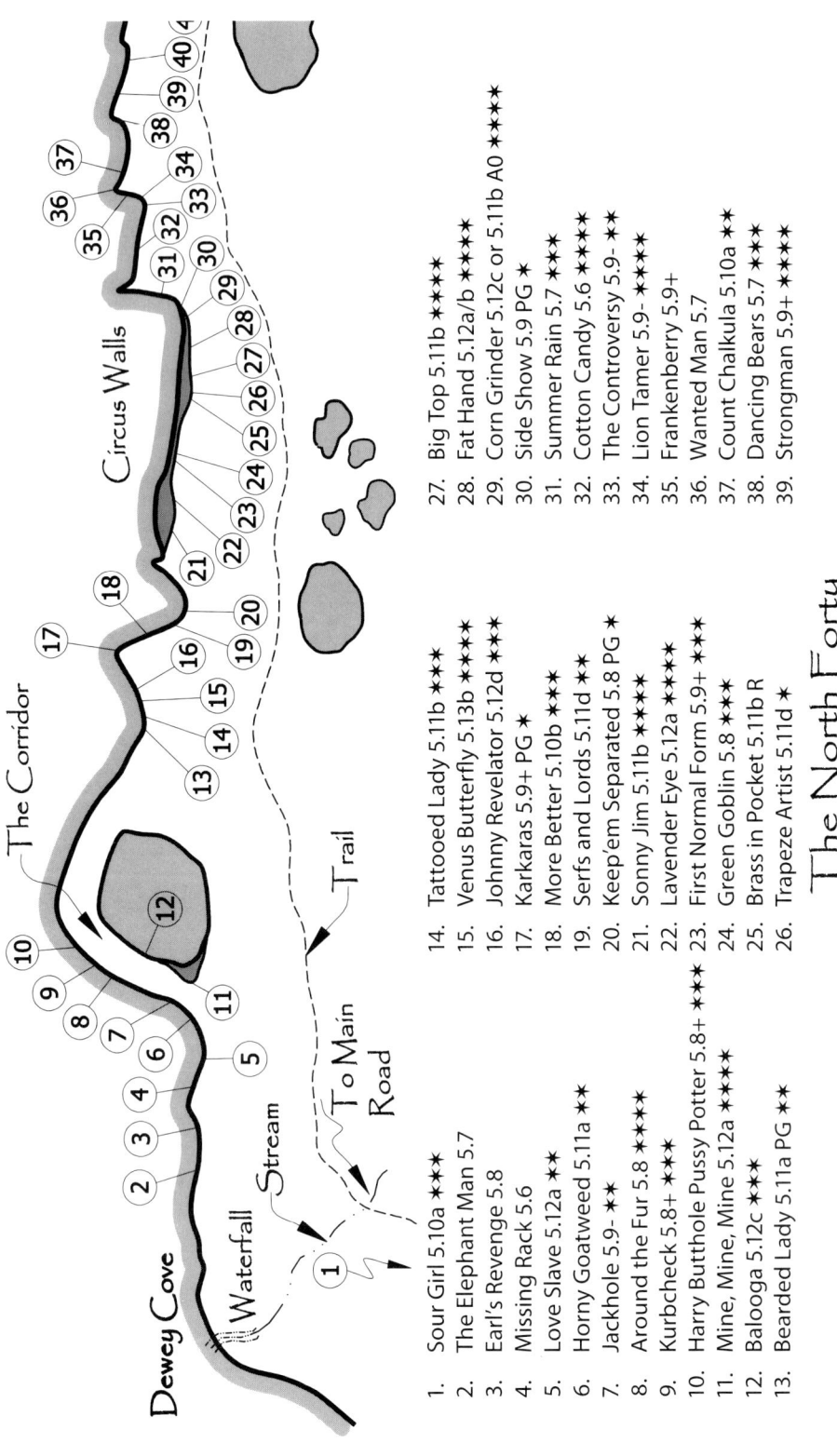

1. Sour Girl 5.10a ★★★
2. The Elephant Man 5.7
3. Earl's Revenge 5.8
4. Missing Rack 5.6
5. Love Slave 5.12a ★★
6. Horny Goatweed 5.11a ★★
7. Jackhole 5.9- ★★
8. Around the Fur 5.8 ★★★★
9. Kurbcheck 5.8+ ★★★
10. Harry Butthole Pussy Potter 5.8+ ★★★★
11. Mine, Mine, Mine 5.12a ★★★★
12. Balooga 5.12c ★★★
13. Bearded Lady 5.11a PG ★★
14. Tattooed Lady 5.11b ★★★
15. Venus Butterfly 5.13b ★★★★
16. Johnny Revelator 5.12d ★★★
17. Karkaras 5.9+ PG ★
18. More Better 5.10b ★★★
19. Serfs and Lords 5.11d ★★
20. Keep'em Separated 5.8 PG ★
21. Sonny Jim 5.11b ★★★★
22. Lavender Eye 5.12a ★★★★
23. First Normal Form 5.9+ ★★★
24. Green Goblin 5.8 ★★★
25. Brass in Pocket 5.11b R
26. Trapeze Artist 5.11d ★
27. Big Top 5.11b ★★★★
28. Fat Hand 5.12a/b ★★★★
29. Corn Grinder 5.12c or 5.11b A0 ★★★★
30. Side Show 5.9 PG ★
31. Summer Rain 5.7 ★★★
32. Cotton Candy 5.6 ★★★★
33. The Controversy 5.9- ★★
34. Lion Tamer 5.9- ★★★★
35. Frankenberry 5.9+
36. Wanted Man 5.7
37. Count Chalkula 5.10a ★★
38. Dancing Bears 5.7 ★★★
39. Strongman 5.9+ ★★★★

The North Forty

2. The Elephant Man 5.7
From **Sour Girl**, cross the creek and head straight for the bluff. This route is a wide dihedral crack. (trad w/o anchors) 35 ft.
FA: Jason Sapp '03

3. Earl's Revenge 5.8
This dihedral cracked is marked by the small tree growing out of it. (trad w/o anchors) 35 ft.
FA: Brandon Jenkins '03

4. Missing Rack 5.6
Climb the short dihedral that starts as a thin seam and widens to a chimney. (trad w/o anchors) 35 ft.
FA: Brandon Jenkins '03

5. Love Slave 5.12a ✷✷
This recent addition is the steep overhanging roof route that starts twenty feet left of **Horny Goatweed**. (5 bolts) 50 ft.
FA: Chad Watkins '05

6. Horny Goatweed 5.11a ✷✷
Walk the bluff or the trail from the creek crossing and look for the large detached block. This route starts on the main bluff left of the mouth of **The Corridor**. Climb right to left up the overhang to the first bolt. A long reach or dynamic move lands you on a nice shelf. Climb just left and then straight up over a small bulge and through a shallow dihedral to good holds. (5 bolts) 50 ft.
FA: Chad Watkins '02

7. Jackhole 5.9- ✷✷
Fifteen feet right of **Horny Goatweed**, climb up a steep start on jugs over a bulge to a stance. Continue up to the roof/bulge and climb on through the crux to the anchors. (4 bolts) 45 ft.
FA: Chad Watkins '02

8. Around the Fur 5.8 ✷✷✷✷
Just five feet right of **Jackhole**, climb up to the twin jugs and a tree. Pull through and stand up to clip the anchors on this fun route. (4 bolts) 45 ft.
FA: Jason Roy '02

9. Kurbcheck 5.8+ ✷✷✷
Move right another five feet past **Around the Fur** and start this climb on thin holds to a break. Continue on good holds to the anchors. (4 bolts) 45 ft.
FA: Kirby McCoy '02

10. Harry Butthole Pussy Potter 5.8+ ✷✷✷
Go yet another five feet right to start on small holds with somewhat technical moves. Climb to the break and the holds get much bigger. (5 bolts) 45 ft.
FA: Chad Watkins '03

11. Mine, Mine, Mine 5.12a ✷✷✷✷
On the low end of the block, climb the overhanging face/arête up and left to the roof. Move left at the roof to the hanging dihedral. Negotiate the crux and move on to the detached flake. Climb the flake to anchors. (5 bolts) 50 ft.
FA: Chad Watkins '02

12. Balooga 5.12c ★★★
Eight feet left of **Mine, Mine, Mine**, stick-clip the first bolt and begin with a boulder problem to the roof. Toss over the lip from crimps to a sloping jug. Mantle and complete the steep headwall on crimps, then finish on pumpy slopers. (5 bolts) 50 ft.
FA: Chad Watkins '03

13. Bearded Lady 5.11a PG ★★
From **The Corridor**, move along the bluff line east about fifty yards. Climb the broken dihedral to an arête. This climb is harder than it looks. (trad w/anchors) 55 ft.
FA: Chad Davis '02

14. Tattooed Lady 5.11b ★★★
Just around the corner from **Bearded Lady**, climb the obvious hand/fist crack to the break. From here, either escape left or attempt the classic gritstone style direct finish. A #5 Camalot for the large pod and a #0 TCU for the direct finish work great. (trad w/anchors) 55 ft.
FA: Chad Davis '02

15. Venus Butterfly 5.13b ★★★★
Just to the right of **Tattooed Lady** is a striking orange bolted line with no holds. This route is yet another of the Unabomber's legacy. (5 bolts) 50 ft.
FA: Nathaniel Walker '02

16. Johnny Revelator 5.12d ★★★
Slightly uphill and right of **Venus Butterfly**, climb the black streak on small holds with powerful moves. (5 bolts) 50 ft.
FA: Chad Watkins '02

17. Karkaras 5.9+ PG ★
Stem up the thin, short dihedral to the right of **Johnny Revelator**. (trad w/o anchors) 35 ft.
FA: Todd Johnson '03

18. More Better 5.10b ★★★
Start on good holds up to a stance. From here, climb some technical face moves avoiding the sometimes wet holds on the left. Have a more better day! (6 bolts) 55 ft.
FA: Chad Watkins '03

19. Serfs and Lords 5.11d ★★
Drop down into the notch to start this route. Climb up and over a bulge to a stance. From here, yank on sloping sidepulls and underclings to reach the break. It can be done static. The crux can also be circumnavigated by traversing left, then up and back right to the bolt line. (6 bolts) 55 ft.
FA: Chad Watkins '03

20. Keep'em Separated 5.8 PG ★
Six feet right of **Serfs and Lords**, start up the short, broken crack system trending left and continue where you find gear. (trad, shares anchors) 55 ft.
FA: Chad Davis '02

21. Sonny Jim 5.11b ★★★★
Round the corner right of **Keep'em Separated** to find a striking orange face capped by a large roof. Start on the left side of the wall behind the boulder. Begin on jugs and move up to a break. Climb onto the blank face above on small holds (some cheat out right to do this) and pull up to sloper crimps. Clip and continue on good holds to the slab section below the roof. Move into the slab on small holds and reach for the plate in the ceiling. Pull out to the lip and haul jugs to the top. (7 bolts) 60 ft.
FA: Chad Watkins '02

Rhonda Watkins climbing Green Goblin

Tom Hancock on Big Top

22. Lavender Eye 5.12a ★★★★
It's just a step to the right, put you hands on your hips, and climb easy moves to the "eye". Pull in and out of the "eye" and up to a stance, then one tricky move and you're at the roof. Negotiate the crux and you are rewarded with jugs to the top. (8 bolts) 65 ft.
FA: Chad Watkins '02

23. First Normal Form 5.9+ ★★★
This is a superb face climb on good holds up to a hanging dihedral. This was originally a great trad route but the Ranch was to be a sport crag, so it was retroed. (9 bolts) 65 ft.
FA: Chad Davis '02

24. Green Goblin 5.8 ★★★
This also was a trad route that was given bolts. Start in the shallow dihedral and climb up and slightly right to continue in the upper dihedral. Go through a slight crux at mid height and you're on to jugs at the top. (9 bolts) 65 ft.
FA: Tom Hancock '02

25. Brass in Pocket 5.11b R
This route has seen only one known ascent. It shares the start with **Trapeze Artist** and moves left on small holds. Plug a tiny brass stopper in the pocket and lunge for the shelf. Continue to the top on jugs. (trad w/o anchors) 65 ft.
FA: Harrison Shull '02

26. Trapeze Artist 5.11d ★
Start by high-stepping onto a jug. Climb up to a break and pull out the small roof onto small holds. Then set up and dyno for the sandwich-shaped block up right -- a long move for anyone. After this, climb on jugs to the top. (7 bolts) 65 ft.
FA: Chad Davis '02

27. Big Top 5.11b ★★★★
This one shares the start with **Trapeze Artist** as well. Pull onto starting holds and trend right to the small roof. Pull out the roof on good holds up to the flexible dinner plate. Move just left off the plate to smaller black holds. Move up and right onto more black holds and then straight to the top. This route was originally done on gear with only the first and third bolts. It was a much different route standing on the flexing dinner plate above a .75 quadcam stuffed into a horizontal. (7 bolts) 65 ft.
FA: Chad Davis '02

28. Fat Hand 5.12a/b ★★★★
A few feet right of **Big Top**, start on the left edge of the cave. Bouldery moves past the first bolt lead to a stance. Move up and right on perfect, incut holds to the bulge/roof and crux. Climb into the fat hand jam and onto the jugs above. This climb is considered by many to be the best line on the wall. (8 bolts) 65 ft.
FA: Chad Davis '02

29. Corn Grinder 5.12c or 5.11b A0 ★★★★
Step up onto the boulder and clip the first bolt. Pull up on the minute holds and fire for more small holds to gain the break (or A0 the first bolt). From here, keep pulling on great stone to the dihedral. Set up and deadpoint to the crack and clip. The rest is gravy. Bon Apetit! (9 bolts) 70 ft.
FA: Chad Watkins '02

30. Side Show 5.9 PG ★
Start right of the boulder on the overhang and climb the blunt arête up and left to the anchors of **Corn Grinder**. (trad, shares anchors) 70 ft.
FA: Chad Davis '02

31. Summer Rain 5.7 ★★★
Around the corner right of **Side Show**, climb a winding route on black stone with enormous holds. The first ascent was done in the rain. A more direct variation departs the original line at mid height and heads to the rightmost set of anchors. (7 bolts) 65 ft.
FA: Chad Watkins '02

32. Cotton Candy 5.6 ★★★★
Right of the dihedral, high-step onto the route and climb straight up on good holds to some cotton candy-sized chickenheads. (8 bolts) 65 ft.
FA: Tom Hancock '02

33. The Controversy 5.9- ★★
This route caused contention for some time on whether or not to bolt it, but it was eventually bolted and the controversy ended. Start on the overhang and pull up to the left side of the arête. Simply follow the bolts. (7 bolts) 65 ft.
FA: Unknown

34. Lion Tamer 5.9- ★★★★
Start on the right side of the arête and climb quality stone to the anchors. (7 bolts) 65 ft.
FA: Chad Davis '02

35. Frankenberry 5.9+
Step right of **Lion Tamer** towards the dihedral and climb up and left to a small roof. Pull over the roof and continue straight to top (7 bolts) 65 ft.
FA: Chad Watkins '02

36. Wanted Man 5.7
Climb the dihedral crack. (trad w/o anchors) 60 ft.
FA: Unknown

37. Count Chalkula 5.10a ★★
To the right of the dihedral, this climb features a tough start with much easier climbing above. (5 bolts) 55 ft.
FA: Chad Watkins '02

38. Dancing Bears 5.7 ★★★
From **Count Chalkula**, walk right up the hill and around the corner to find the wide dihedral on black rock. This is a fun climb that protects well. (trad w/anchors) 50 ft.
FA: Unknown

39. Strongman 5.9+ ★★★★
Start five feet right of the black dihedral and test your strength on the bouldery start of this wonderful climb. Once you have passed the test, continue on gorgeous jugs to the top. (6 bolts) 50 ft.
FA: Chad Davis '02

40. The Greatest Show on Earth 5.8+ ★★★★
This is a classic that everyone should do. As with most Chad Davis moderates, the first ascent was a solo. Climb a difficult but enjoyable start on black rock to perfect Arkansas style jugs. (5 bolts) 50 ft.
FA: Chad Davis '02

Chad Davis on the first ascent of Strongman

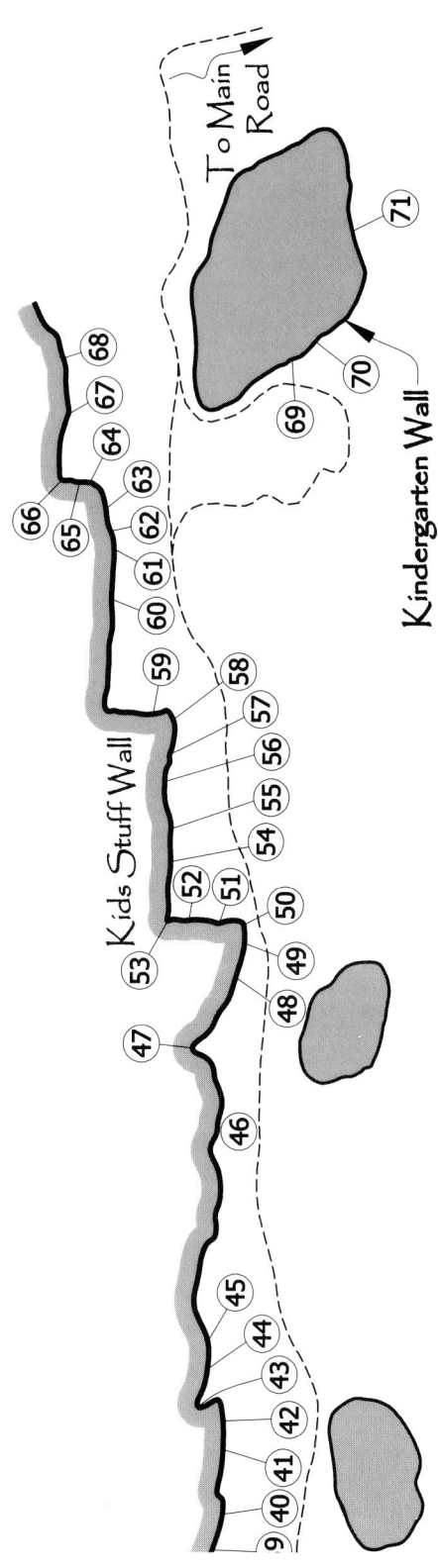

40. The Greatest Show on Earth 5.8+ ★★★★
41. Circus Freaks 5.9- PG ★
42. African Herbman 5.8+ ★★★★
43. Clown Suit 5.8
44. Mr. Hanky 5.10d ★★
45. Petrified 5.12a ★★
46. Webster's Part 5.6 ★★★
47. Poetry in Goshen 5.9 PG
48. Private Property 5.10a ★★★
   VARIATION: Lamb Chops 5.9 PG
49. Crimp Scampi 5.10d ★★★

50. Leonid 5.9+ ★★★
51. Girth Hitch 5.7 ★★★
52. Local Hebrew 5.9- ★★★
53. Zeppelin 5.7
54. Little Manly Man 5.7 ★★
55. Tunnel Vision 5.7 ★
56. Sundial 5.7 ★★★
57. Kid's Stuff 5.6
58. Molt 5.8+ ★★★
59. Tres Equis 5.8 ★★★
60. The Bulb 5.8 ★★★★

61. Sons of the Soil 5.10a ★★
62. Groove Tube 5.8+ PG
63. Groovy 5.8 ★★★
64. Newton County Mentality 5.11a ★★★
65. Brand New 5.8 ★★
66. Narwhal 5.7 ★
67. Cows in the Mist 5.7 ★★★
68. Emma's Got a Mullet 5.7 ★★
69. Guide Route 5.5 ★★
70. Guide Route 5.5 ★★
71. Crab Louse 5.12a/b PG ★

The North Forty

54 • *The North Forty*

41. Circus Freaks 5.9- PG ✱
Start on **African Herbman** and follow the path of least resistance and most pro. A 5.7 variation starts further to the left and then trends back right to the original line. (trad shares anchors) 50 ft.
FA: Chad Davis '02

42. African Herbman 5.8+ ✱✱✱✱
This is the classic line at the right end of the wall. Climb just left of the arête on jugs to the first bolt. Technical moves up to the second bolt are followed by easier but steeper climbing on jugs. (6 bolts) 55 ft.
FA: Chad Watkins '02

43. Clown Suit 5.8
Climb the short, off-width dihedral. (trad w/o anchors) 45 ft.
FA: Unknown

44. Mr. Hanky 5.10d ✱✱
Right of the dihedral, climb a tough start from the left to the center of the wall. The original route stayed right of the jugs and ascended small holds separated by long reaches, but most climbers opt to stay left on the larger holds. (4 bolts) 40 ft.
FA: Chad Watkins '02

45. Petrified 5.12a ✱✱
This route starts right and moves left into the center, joining **Mr. Hanky** for the last bolt and anchors. A bouldery start on shallow pockets leads up to crimps and left to jugs. (4 bolts) 40 ft.
FA: Chad Watkins '02

46. Webster's Part 5.6 ✱✱✱
Seventy yards right of **Petrified**, start right of the small pine tree and climb to the odd bulge at the top. (6 bolts) 40 ft.
FA: Chad Watkins '02

47. Poetry in Goshen 5.9 PG
This is the overhanging off-width to the right of **Webster's**. (trad w/o anchors) 45 ft.
FA: Unknown

48. Private Property 5.10a ✱✱✱
Start on the detached flake and climb left to the face. Continue straight up over a bulge, and climb to the top on good holds. (6 bolts) 55 ft.
FA: Chad Watkins '03

   VARIATION: Lamb Chops 5.9 PG
Climb the flake and continue trending up and left on gear. (trad w/o anchors) 55 ft.
FA: Misty Lamb '02

49. Crimp Scampi 5.10d ✱✱✱✱
Climb the obvious stellar face on classic chocolatey orange stone. Don't lose a finger in the lock. (5 bolts) 55 ft.
FA: Chad Watkins '02

50. Leonid 5.9+ ✱✱✱
This is the arête just right of **Crimp Scampi**. A difficult start leads to moderate climbing above. This is a classic that everyone should do. (6 bolts) 55 ft.
FA: Chad Davis '02

51. Girth Hitch 5.7 ✱✱✱
This is the route eight feet right of **Leonid** on black stone. (5 bolts) 50 ft.
FA: Chad Davis '02

52. Local Hebrew 5.9- ★★★
Start just five feet left of the dihedral, and enjoy good climbing with a slight crux in the middle. (5 bolts) 45 ft.
FA: Chad Watkins '02

53. Zeppelin 5.7
The is yet another dihedral crack. (trad w/o anchors) 45 ft.
FA: Unknown

54. Little Manly Man 5.7 ★★
Ten feet right of the dihedral, start on an obvious high-step. Thin holds lead to bigger ones and a break. Climb into the thin right-facing dihedral and continue to the top. (5 bolts) 45 ft.
FA: Chad Watkins '02

55. Tunnel Vision 5.7 ★
Start just right of the small tree with reachy moves and trend slightly left and up to a large ledge. From here, look hard to find the good holds to the top. (5 bolts) 45 ft.
FA: Chad Watkins '02

56. Sundial 5.7 ★★★
Start ten feet right of **Tunnel Vision** on small holds to a break. Enormous holds carry you to the top. (5 bolts) 45 ft.
FA: Chad Watkins '02

57. Kid's Stuff 5.6
Five feet right of **Sundial**, climb the shallow dihedral/face to anchors. (trad w/anchors) 45 ft.
FA: Chad Watkins '02

58. Molt 5.8+ ★★★
Start on jugs in a shallow corner just left of the blunt arête. Move up to bigger holds and then onto the slab with thin moves to the top. (5 bolts) 40 ft.
FA Chad Watkins '02

59. Tres Equis 5.8 ★★★
Eight feet right of the arête, start on good holds. Climb past the break to a stance, and then up tricky moves to the top. (3 bolts) 35 ft.
FA: Chad Watkins '02

60. The Bulb 5.8 ★★★
Start on a detached flake forty feet right of a dihedral. Climb sidepulls and crimps to better holds, and finish on the obvious bulb. This is a fun climb. (5 bolts) 40 ft.
FA: Chad Watkins '02

61. Sons of the Soil 5.10a ★★
Start eight feet right of **The Bulb** on thin moves over a bulge. Continue on jugs. (5 bolts) 40 ft.
FA: Jason Roy '02

62. Groove Tube 5.8+ PG
Climb the wide dihedral. (trad w/o anchors) 40 ft.
FA: Unknown

63. Groovy 5.8 ★★★
Start at the left edge of the cave. High-step onto good holds, and move right into worm grooves. Continue up to jugs and easy climbing to the top. (5 bolts) 45 ft.
FA: Chad Watkins '02

Singer/Songwriter Dallas Jones pondering First Normal Form

64. Newton County Mentality 5.11a ★★★
On the east side of the cave, step up on cheater stones to reach the starting holds. Power up and right to a sidepull and crimp. Pull into the shallow dihedral, climb to the hanging arête and continue to the top. (6 bolts) 45 ft.
FA: Jason Roy '02

65. Brand New 5.8 ★★
This is the nice face climb just right of **Newton County Mentality**. (5 bolts) 45 ft.
FA: Chad Watkins '05

66. Narwhal 5.7 ★
Climb the chimney in the dihedral to the right of **Brand New**. (trad w/anchors) 40 ft.
FA: Chad Davis '02

67. Cows in the Mist 5.7 ★★★
This is the fun jug climb to the right of **Narwhal.** (4 bolts) 40 ft.
FA: Chad Davis '02

68. Emma's Got a Mullet 5.7 ★★
Further to the right, climb the slabby dihedral. (4 bolts) 40 ft.
FA: Jason Roy '05

69. Guide Route 5.5 ★★
Jug climb on the **Kindergarten Boulder** (trad w/anchors) 35 ft.
FA: Unknown

70. Guide Route 5.5 ★★
Jug climb on the **Kindergarten Boulder** (trad w/anchors) 35 ft.
FA: Unknown

71. Crab Louse 5.12a/b PG ★
On the south end of the **Kindergarten Boulder**, pull powerful moves up the steep face. Take care not to blow the clips! (3 bolts) 30 ft.
FA: Chad Watkins '02

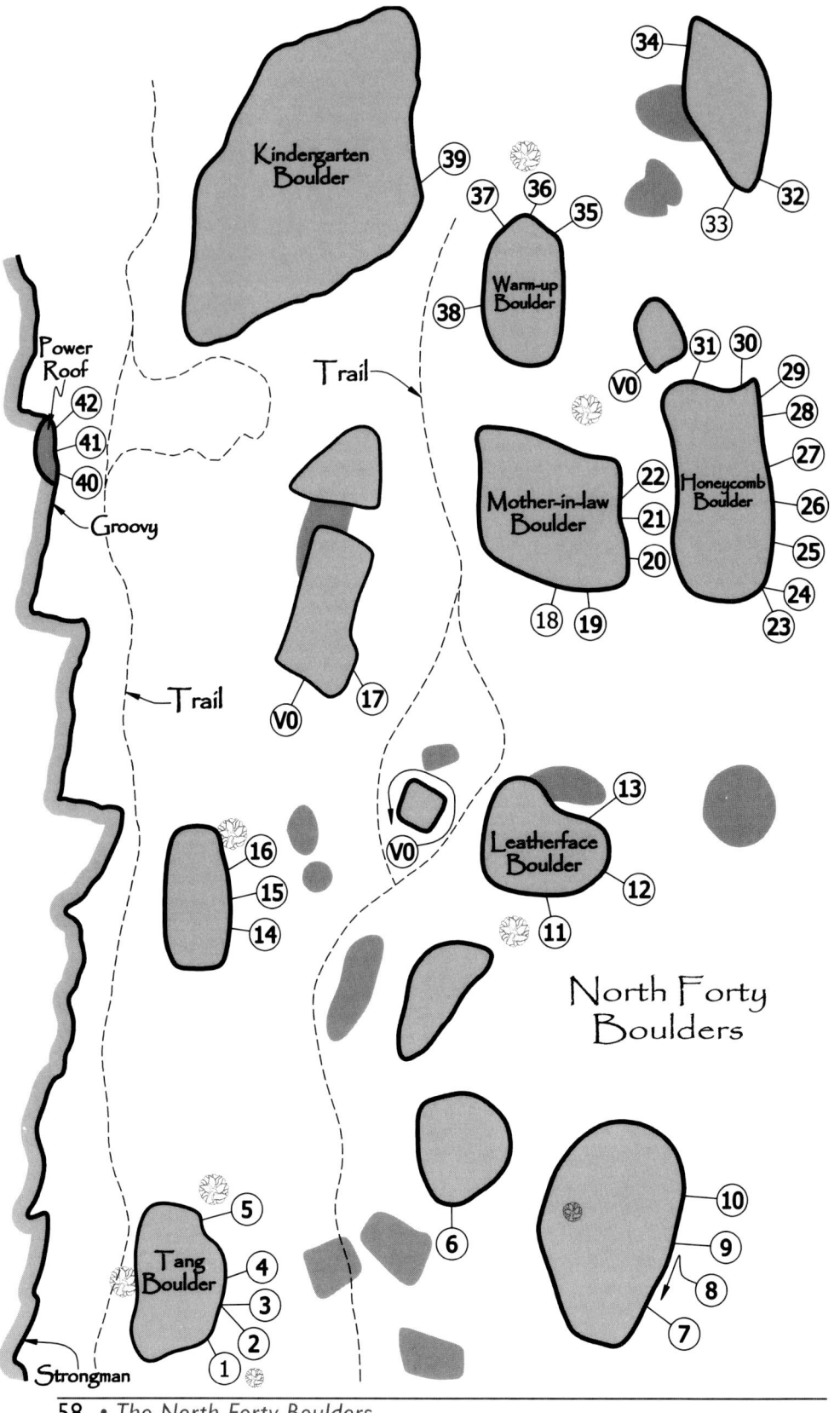

The **North Forty** also offers a fine collection of boulder problems on the boulders below the cliff line. There are more problems that are not listed but here are a few to get you started.

1. **Pilsnergeist V1** - Climb up face.
2. **Crack Ho V2** - Lieback the crack.
3. **Orb Weaver V7** - SDS **Crack Ho** and follow to finish of **Tang**.
4. **Tang V10** - Stand Start on sidepulls and climb face on crimps.
5. **Cosmic Sensorship V7** - SDS with a gaston and shallow sidepull pocket.
6. **Broken V3** - Arête with pockets.
7. **Toe Poke V5** - Left hand sloper, right hand sloper, throw to sloper.
8. **Linkup V?** - Link **Eunuch** into **Toe Poke**.
9. **Eunuch V5** - Crimp to jugs, highball.
10. **Clever French Footwork V4** - Choose some pockets.
11. **A Little More John Wayne V4** - SDS on tooth, move left and up.
12. **Leather Face V7** - SDS and move out roof on crimps and move right to top-out.
13. **Chainsaw V4** - SDS on a small boulder, head for top, bad landing.
14. **Bad Daze V5** - SDS on crimps, climb face on crimps and top-out right.
15. **Better Daze V5** - SDS on rail and finish on **Bad Daze**.
16. **Best Daze V6** - SDS under roof and climb face left of arête.
17. **The Ramp V3** - Scary highball slab.
18. **Butt Cradle V3** - SDS, traverse left to seam and top-out on slopers.
19. **Toilet Bowl V2** - SDS in the bowl and climb up to sloper top-out.
20. **Short Subject V3** - SDS to good mantle.
21. **Fiber Con V4** - SDS below dihedral to the sloping shelf, go left.
22. **Mother-in-law V5** - SDS on bad holds and move up arête.
23. **Honeycomb Traverse V6** - Start on left side and traverse right across face.
24. **GGF V3** - SDS, move up to large blunt arête.
25. **36DD's V3** - SDS up crimps and top-out on the D-cup sized slopers.
26. **Slapstick V4** - Start on crimps and move up to sloper top-out.
27. **Uncle Fister V4** - Start on crimps and finish on fist crack.
28. **Hulsey Did It V3** - SDS on crimps and move up to odd knob, finish in notch.
29. **The End V3** - SDS, climb over bulge to slopey top-out.
30. **High Rise Penthouse V4** - SDS on good holds to steep face, finish on slab.
31. **The Beginning V2** - Stand start and climb steep wall.
32. **Trouser Chili V4** - SDS sloper arete to top.
33. **Glory Hole V4** - SDS in the hole, avoid the arete.
34. **Chasing Demons V3** - Highball on good pockets.
35. **Think French V2** - Sidepull and bad sloper to top.
36. **Nude Beach V1** - Stand start and climb juggy face to slopey top-out.
37. **Easy Peasy V0** - Stand start on good holds and continue to easy finish.
38. **Perpetual Motion Machine V4** - Traverse left and top-out **Think French**.
39. **Static Tang V6** - SDS up bad crimps to jugs move left and drop off at the jug.
40. **Render V5** - SDS on jug, climb out roof and top-out over lip.
41. **Kneeling Before Power V9** - Start in back of roof seam, climb out on sidepulls and move right and out to lip.
42. **Orbital Mechanics V8** - SDS to right of **Kneeling Before Power** on crimps. Continue out roof on sidepulls and crimps to top-out over lip.

Mike Wintroath on an early attempt of his Respect My Authority Photo: Spencer Tirey

The Goat Cave is the perfect outdoor gym for those who like to get inverted. Though the routes here are not long, they offer a vicious pump. The most popular climbs are on the right side of the cave. The others, while still steep, are painfully crimpy and have more powerfully defined cruxes. This makes them no less fun, but only less traveled. Recommended climbs include **Respect My Authority** simply because it is pure fun. **Austrian Ass Attack** is another, but they are all good. Summer climbing is warm, but the sun is high in the sky, so you're shaded. In the winter, the low position of the sun warms you nicely.

To find this area, drive or hike back out the ranch road to the turnoff on the east side of the road with the "RANCH VEHICLES ONLY" sign. Park, without blocking the way, and hike the logging road to a "Y". Follow the left option up a steep hill to a footpath, and hike past the cookout area. At the left end of the zip-line you will find the trail. Follow this to the cave.

1.   Shits and Giggles 5.12c ✶
This is the route at the left edge of the cave without fixed draws. Start off the large boulder and climb to the roof. Move right on medium holds to the flat roof and climb straight out the roof on a thin flake to a lip. Pull the lip to reach anchors. (5 bolts) 45 ft.
FA: Nathaniel Walker '03

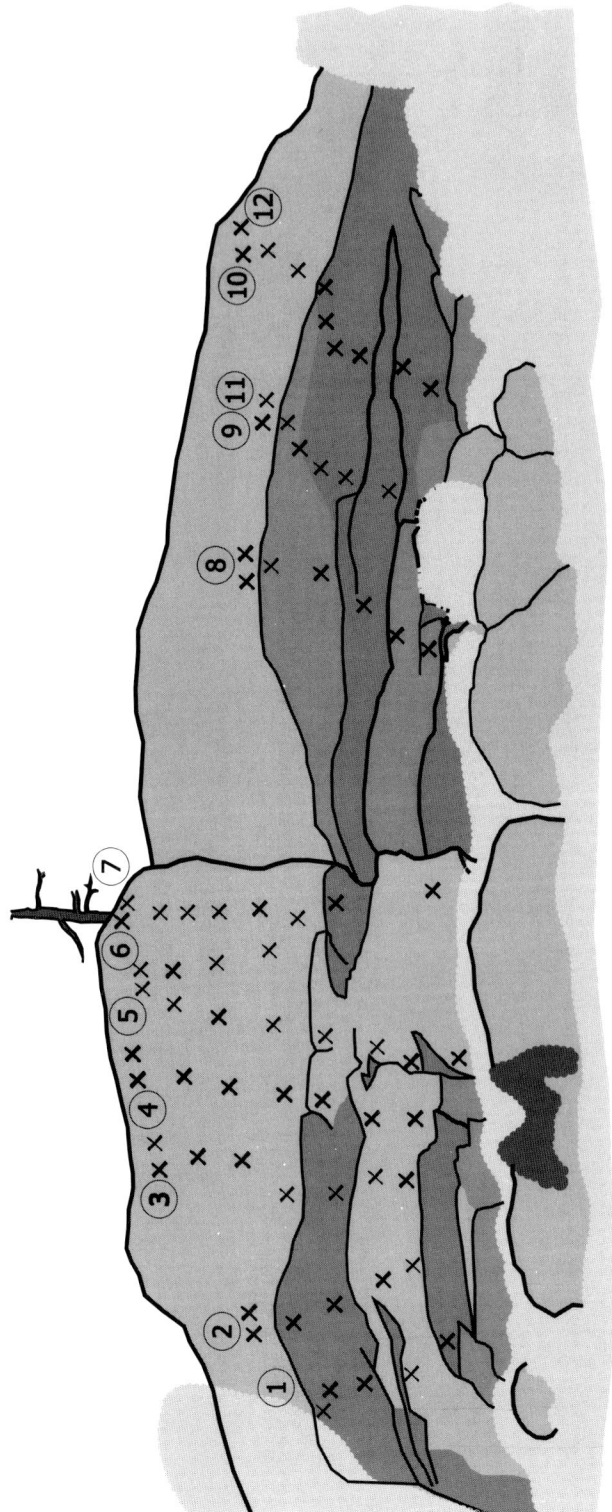

1. Shits and Giggles 5.12c ★
2. Dirty Trip 5.12b/c ★★
3. Greasy Kid's Stuff 5.12a ★★
4. Anal Sac Expression 5.10d ★★★
5. Austrian Ass Attack 5.12a ★★★★
6. Mexican Sac Pull 5.11a/b ★★★★
7. PBR 5.11a/b ★★★★
8. Man Junk 5.12b ★★★★
9. Junk Bus 5.12b ★★★
10. Flabby Armed Spanking Machine 5.12c/d ★★★★
11. Ride the Short Bus 5.12b ★★★
12. Respect My Authority 5.12c ★★★★

The Goat Cave

2. Dirty Trip 5.12b/c ★★
Start off the boulder and pull up to a tough boulder problem before the roof. Jugs at the roof set you up for the long reach to a bad pinch. Pull the pinch to your chest and reach for the jug, continue left to the anchors. (fixed) 45 ft.
FA: Chad Watkins '03

3. Greasy Kid's Stuff 5.12a ★★
Start again off the boulder and pull into another boulder problem start. Pull up to the roof and jugs. From the jugs, pull up to a thin undercling and a sidepull. Toss for a jug, and continue over the lip to the headwall, and up to the anchors. (6 bolts/3 fixed) 50 ft.
FA: Kerry Allen '02

4. Anal Sac Expression 5.10d ★★★
Stick-clip, then start off the right edge of the boulder. Pull onto medium holds to gain the roof. Move out the roof on good holds and pull over the lip onto large plates. Then move right a little and climb straight up the headwall on sloping holds. (6 bolts) 55 ft.
FA: Chad Watkins '03

5. Austrian Ass Attack 5.12a ★★★★
Start in the overhanging hand/fist crack and climb out to the chockstone. Continue trending right on jugs to find the crux at two-thirds height. Pull through the crux on slopers with a mean pump. Continue to anchors or drop off at the last bolt. (fixed) 55 ft.
FA: Chad Watkins '02

6. Mexican Sac Pull 5.11a/b ★★★★
Start twelve feet right of the corner with a hanging start on jugs. Climb up into a small cave, move left out of the cave and onto jugs, and climb these jugs to a small roof. Then pull over the lip and into the crux. Negotiate the crux and control the pump and you might get to the anchors. (6 bolts) 50 ft.
FA: Chad Watkins '02

7. PBR 5.11a/b ★★★★
Climb **Mexican Sac Pull** until the third bolt, and then move right onto jugs. Climb a wandering line with some technical moves to reach the top. (6 bolts) 50 ft.
FA: Chris French '02

8. Man Junk 5.12b ★★★★
Twenty-five feet right of **PBR**, stick-clip and start off cheater stones on crimp-jugs and heel hooks. Deadpoint right to a sloping pinch. Then figure out what to do next to gain the stance in the dihedral to the left. Pull up to the break and move right to the roof. At the roof, pull straight out to crimp-jugs and make a long move to a jug. Pull past the jug to sloping jug pockets and the anchors. (fixed) 50 ft.
FA: Chad Watkins '02

9. Junk Bus 5.12b ★★★
Climb the first three bolts of **Man Junk** and traverse into the final rail of **Ride the Short Bus**. (fixed) 50 ft.
FA: Chad Watkins '04

10. Flabby Armed Spanking Machine 5.12c/d ★★★★
Start on **Man Junk**, and climb through **Short Bus** onto the crux rail of **Respect My Authority**. Continue past the rail for two more bolts to the lip at the right edge of the cave and drop off. (9 bolts w/o anchors) 60 ft.
FA: Chad Watkins '05

A crusty old trad climber keeps watch

11. Ride the Short Bus 5.12b ✶✶✶
Start off of a boulder right of **Man Junk**. Stick-clip your rope high. Campus or try to find feet and pull from a crimp-rail to a crimp in the short dihedral overhead. Reach past a crimp to a jug and paste your feet. Climb jugs to the right out the roof to the lip. Move slightly left at the lip and throw for a sloper then match and move right to the anchors. (fixed) 50 ft.
FA: Chad Watkins '02

12. Respect My Authority 5.12c ✶✶✶✶
This is the rightmost route in the cave. Start in the back of the cave in a thin dihedral. Lieback to the first roof and then move out right to the lip. Pull over the lip to small holds and fire left for a jug. Find the hand jam rest and clip. Reach over the block to another jug. From the jugs, reach out to a pocket jug, a rail, and then a flake, to the lip. Pull the lip (the redpoint crux) and go on to anchors. (fixed) 55 ft.
FA: Mike Wintroath '03

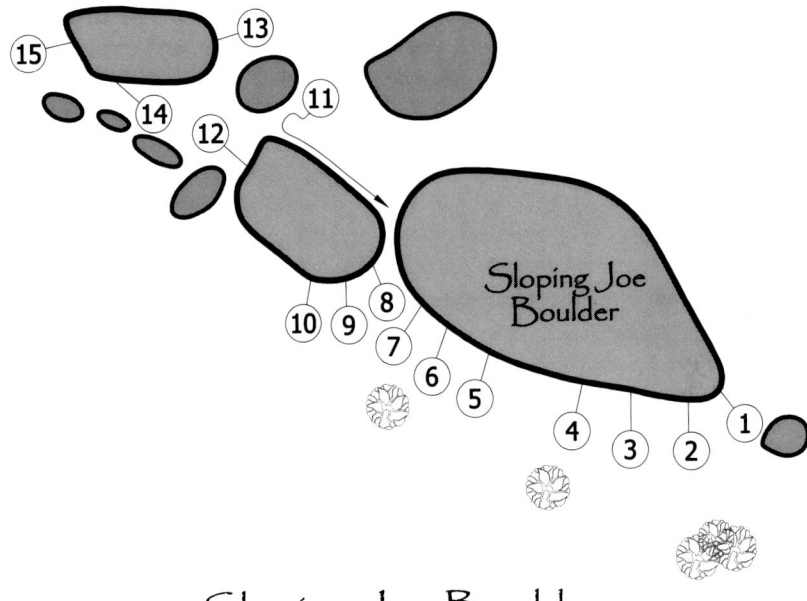

Sloping Joe Boulders

The Sloping Joe Boulders are a wonderful little collection of just high enough boulder problems. They can be found on the left side of the approach trail to **The Goat Cave**, just before the steep footpath leading up to the cookout area. It is a great place to boulder in the dead of winter.

1. **Trees, Shrubs, and Vines V2** - Jugs and cracks to a sloper top-out.
2. **Wildflowers V3** - More jugs and cracks to a sloper top-out.
3. **Slopadon Milosevic V5** - Water groove to a good pinch.
4. **Le Surprise V5** - Start on the broken hold, go to crimp, toss for sloper, and then trend left.
5. **Choosing Sides V6** - Start on two sidepulls, crimps to top-out.
6. **Lead Better Wedding V5** - SDS to a good rail, finish on sloper top-out.
7. **Sloping Joe V3** - Mantel on a good jug.
8. **The Dowry V5** - SDS on arête, trend left.
9. **Keep doing problems like this and you will never get sponsored V1** - Slab.
10. **Unnamed Problem V1**
11. **Burnt Out V3** - Slab with slopers on the arête.
12. **Stumpy Butt V4** - SDS on pockets, to good edges, and finish on slopey top-out.
13. **Unnamed Problem V1**
14. **Unnamed Problem V1**
15. **Unnamed Problem V1**

Ingrid Chiles on Party in the Back

MULLET BUTTRESS

Mullet Buttress was one of the first places bolted lines started popping up on the ranch. Among these, Dave McGee gave us the classics **Mixed Max** and **Troubadour**. Not to be left out, **Party in the Back** is a 5.8+ must-do, while **Business in the Front** lives up to its name. **The Mullet** can be unbearable in the summer, as briars tend to take over and it can get rather miserable. That said, winter is the best time to climb in this area.

To find this area, either hike the trail from the cookout area below **The Goat Cave** or approach from the trail leading up to **Land of the Lost**.

1. **Mixed Max 5.11d** ✦✦
On the far left side of the **Troubadour** buttress, climb the steep, shallow dihedral on thin holds. Then climb technical moves to the top. (6 bolts) 50 ft.
FA: Dave McGee '01

2. **Ignatius 5.10c PG** ✦✦✦
On the front of the **Troubadour** buttress, start on jugs and climb straight to the small roof/bulge. Climb out and up to anchors. (trad, shares anchors) 55 ft.
FA: Dave McGee '01

3. **Full Frontal Nudity 5.10c** ✦✦✦
Climb **Ignatius**, but clip the bolts. (5 bolts) 55 ft.
FA: Chad Watkins '02

4. **Troubadour 5.10d** ✦✦✦✦
Step right to the steep arête and climb up and right onto the steep headwall. (5 bolts) 50 ft.
FA: Dave McGee '01

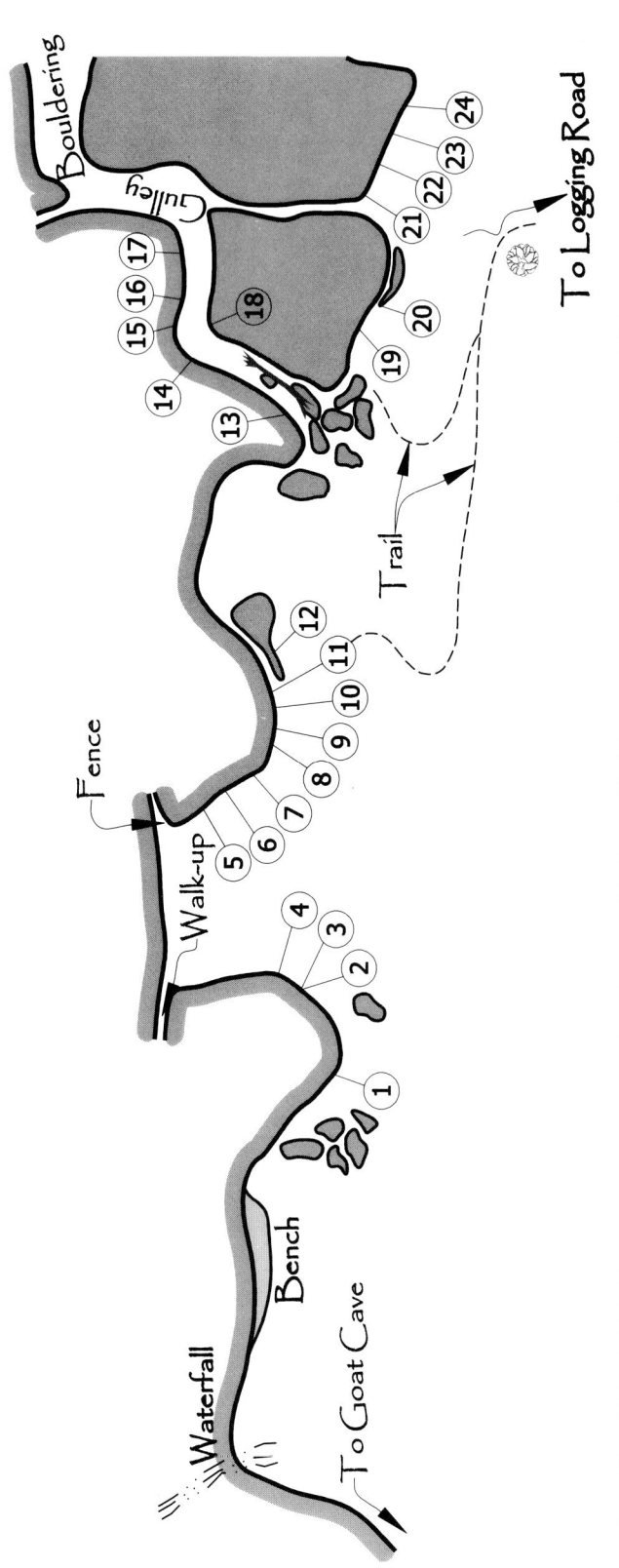

1. Mixed Max 5.11d ★★
2. Ignatius 5.10c PG ★★★
3. Full Frontal Nudity 5.10c ★★★
4. Troubadour 5.10d ★★★★
5. Business in the Front 5.10b ★★★
6. When Mullets Attack 5.9+ R ★★
7. Party in the Back 5.8+ ★★★★
8. Pimp-Ass Midgiemullet 5.11a ★★★
9. Camaro Mullet 5.10b ★★
10. Military Cut 5.10a ★★★
11. Mohawk 5.10a ★★
12. Tongue Lash V4 ★★★
13. Lost Left Sock 5.8 ★★
14. Whiskey River 5.9 PG ★★★
15. Sleestack 5.12b ★★★
16. Jimmy Hoffa 5.12b ★★★
17. Atlantis 5.12a ★★★
18. The Penny Cigarette 5.12a ★★★
19. Killing With Stone V6
20. Stuck in the Middle V6
21. Pride 5.12b ★★
22. Envy 5.13a ★★
23. Hiking Under the Influence 5.10b ★★★
24. Mini-Me 5.10c ★★

Mullet Buttress/Land of Lost

Ingrid Chiles reaches the anchors on Party in the Back

5. Business in the Front 5.10b ✶✶✶
Walk the bluff south to the **Mullet Buttress** and start this route left of center. Climb the steep route on excellent stone. (4 bolts) 45 ft.
FA: Dave McGee '01

6. When Mullets Attack 5.9+ R ✶✶
Climb the center of the buttress. (trad w/o anchors) 45 ft.
FA: Dave McGee '01

7. Party in the Back 5.8+ ✶✶✶✶
This is the bolted line on the right side of the face. It is also an excellent climb on great stone. (5 bolts) 45 ft.
FA: Dave McGee '01

8. Pimp-Ass Midgiemullet 5.11a ✶✶✶
Round the corner to the right of **Party in the Back** and start on either side of the first bolt and continue up the serpentine seam. (6 bolts) 50 ft.
FA: Tom Hancock '02

9. Camaro Mullet 5.10b ✶✶
Start on **Pimp-Ass Midgiemullet**, and then head up the rightmost seam. (TR) 50 ft.
FA: Unknown

10. Military Cut 5.10a ✶✶✶
Right of **Camaro Mullet**, start this great route on thin moves and climb right of the hanging block. (6 bolts) 55 ft.
FA: Jason Roy '02

11. Mohawk 5.10a ✶✶
Start five feet right of **Military Cut** and climb thin, technical moves to the easier ground above. (5 bolts) 55 ft.
FA: Chad Watkins '02

12. Tongue Lash V4 ✶✶✶
SDS and climb crimps to the roof. Then grab the outer edges and iron-cross out to the end and mantle. (BP)
FA: Chad Watkins '02

Kirby McCoy on Pride

Land of the Lost

The Land of the Lost is a hidden gem for those hot July days. The climbs here are hard, with only four routes under 5.12. Located behind a massive boulder, this area sports some powerful routes with stellar movement. **Sleestack** is a sustained area testpiece. Not to be outdone, both **Jimmy Hoffa** and **Atlantis** are very intense routes. While these routes remain shaded most of the day, the remainder of the area's routes lie outside and to the right of the protective boulder. These remaining routes are short but steep and powerful at each respective grade.

To find this area, either hike from the road to **The Goat Cave** or hike the east side logging road that services **Magoo Rock** and **The Tool Buttress**. Once you are halfway between **The Goat Cave** and **The Tool Buttress**, hike straight up the hill two hundred yards and look for a marker on a tree. The trailhead is here. Follow the trail to the wooden sign and into the corridor.

13. Lost Left Sock 5.8 ★★
On the left wall at the opening, climb jugs up the strange formations. (6 bolts) 50 ft.
FA: Chad Watkins '03

14. Whiskey River 5.9 PG ★★★
Go to the back of the corridor and climb the dihedral to a small roof. Move slightly left and proceed through the steep dihedral protected by a bolt. The bolt was added by a subsequent ascent party to eliminate a somewhat dangerous section. (trad w/1 bolt, anchors) 60 ft.
FA: Clay Frisbie '01

15. Sleestack 5.12b ★★★
Start in the dihedral and move right at the second bolt. Climb thin technical moves to a flake-jug. Pull past the flake to small holds and onto the jugs under the roof. Climb straight out the roof on large plates to a lip. Turn the lip on slopers to find more slopers, and stand up to reach the anchors. (8 bolts) 60 ft.
FA: Chad Watkins '02

16. Jimmy Hoffa 5.12b ★★★
Start five feet right of **Sleestack** on a large flake. At the second bolt, set up for a difficult undercling move above your head. Pull slightly right out of the undercling and then back left to a long gaston reach. Pull through this powerful section to reach good holds on the vertical wall above. (6 bolts) 55 ft.
FA: Chad Watkins '02

17. Atlantis 5.12a ★★★
On the arête ten feet right of **Jimmy Hoffa**, stick-clip the first bolt, and then start on small holds and make a difficult move slightly right to a small iron rail. Make a long reach to the sloping dishes above. Pull these down to reach small holds beneath a small piece of a roof. From here, locate the jug under the roof. Move right out of the roof to a sloping rail and climb up the rail to gain a jug. (6 bolts) 55 ft.
FA: Chad Watkins '02

18. The Penny Cigarette 5.12a ★★★
Directly across from the former routes you will find a short blunt arête. Stick-clip, then start on a trending lieback flake to small holds. Pull up right to more small holds. From here, balance straight to the top on sloper-sidepulls and crimps. Mind the barn door at the difficult second clip. (2 bolts) 25 ft.
FA: Chad Watkins '02

19. Killing With Stone V6
Located on the block as you approach the entrance to this area, start with a SDS on overhanging stone ten feet left of the obvious blade. Pull off the ground on tiny holds and deadpoint right to a small hold and match. Pull straight up and continue to the highball top-out. (BP) 25 ft.
FA: Nathaniel Walker '02

20. Stuck in the Middle V6
SDS and climb the blade to the top. (BP) 20 ft.
FA: Nathaniel Walker '02

21. Pride 5.12b ★★
To find this route, either go back out of the corridor and move south along the bluff fifty yards or follow the corridor past **Atlantis** and look right to find a smaller corridor that will take you down and out, right to this route. Located on the north arête, climb bouldery moves all the way up this powerful route. (5 bolts) 45 ft.
FA: Nathaniel Walker '02

22. Envy 5.13a ★★
Start just five feet right of **Pride** with a reach to a jug. Pull up right to small holds, and move slightly left to even smaller holds to set up for the crux. The next move will be difficult for smaller climbers, unless a knee bar is employed. Reach as far as you can, and then reach some more, to gain a hold that will feel like nothing. Pull on this with perfect balance and cross through to another bad hold and stand up to a jug. Easy climbing takes you to the top. (5 bolts) 45 ft.
FA: Nathaniel Walker '02

Eric Hudkins climbing Pimp-Ass Midgiemullet

23. Hiking Under the Influence 5.10b ✶✶✶
Start under the obvious roof on the left side and boulder up to the roof and out to the lip. Pull the lip and continue to the top. (4 bolts) 35 ft.
FA: Kerry Allen '02

24. Mini-Me 5.10c ✶✶
Just right of **Hiking Under the Influence**, climb up to and out the roof. Continue on steep rock to the anchors. (2 bolts) 30 ft.
FA: Chad Watkins '02

Todd Johnson about to discover the crux of Don't Be A Tool

MIDDLE EAST

The Middle East is the loneliest place on the ranch. With only a handful of routes to its name, **The Tool Buttress** is not where everyone is going. If that sounds like the kind of isolated privacy you're looking for, then knock yourself out! The routes are on some of the best stone in the canyon; it's just too bad there are not more. This are is nuclear in the summer but great in the winter. There are also several good boulders below the cliff line to keep the kids occupied.

To find this area, hike south from the **Land of The Lost** along the east side logging road to the obvious trail below the buttress or hike north along the east side logging road from the **East Campground** to the top. Keep moving north fifty yards to the trail that leads up to the buttress.

1.   The Poo-Choo Train 5.11b ✶✶
This is the route at the left end of the wall. Climb crimps to the break, and pull out the roof to the face above. (7 bolts) 65 ft.
FA: Chris French '02

2.   Don't Be A Tool 5.12a ✶✶✶
Climb the crimpy face in the center and set up for a long reach or deadpoint to a good hold. Continue on excellent climbing to the roof, and then pull into the dihedral above and climb to the anchors. (10 bolts) 65 ft.
FA: Kerry Allen '02

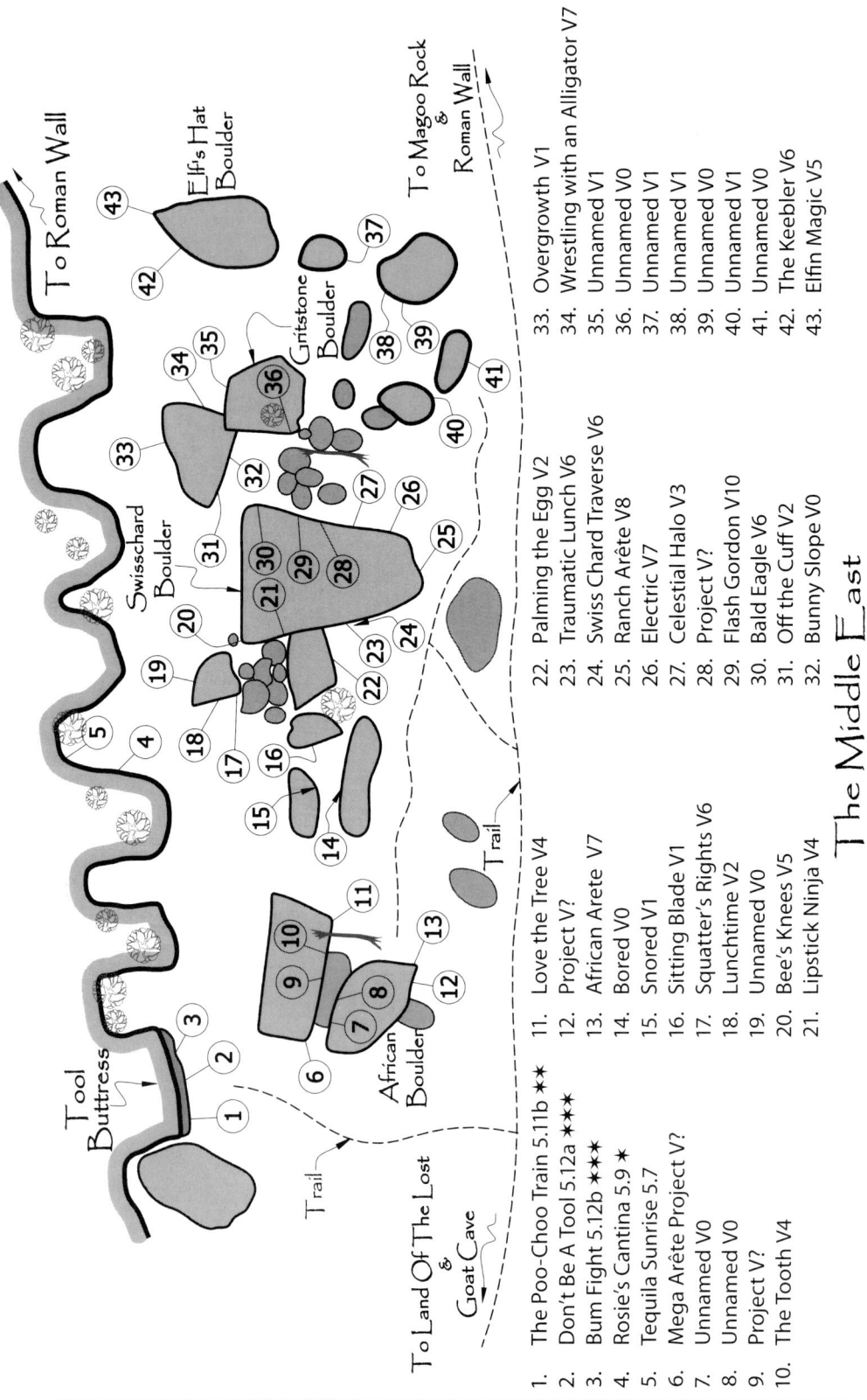

3. **Bum Fight 5.12b** ✶✶✶
At the right end of the wall, climb crimps to the roof. Pull onto the roof flakes, climb out to the lip, and turn onto the face above. (7 bolts) 65 ft.
FA: Mike Wintroath '02

4. **Rosie's Cantina 5.9** ✶
This is the isolated but bolted slab halfway between the **Tool Buttress** and the **Roman Wall**. This route is likely the first bolted sport climb at the Ranch. (4 bolts) 50 ft.
FA: Todd Miller '00

5. **Tequila Sunrise 5.7**
Climb the dihedral crack just right of **Rosie's Cantina.** (trad w/o anchors) 50 ft.
FA: Todd Miller '00

Blake Strickland on the brutishly difficult Mega Arête

An unknown Redbull Redpoint Roundup competitor on Mr. Charlie

MR. MAGOO ROCK ★

Magoo Rock has some of the best lines on the Ranch. The stone is perfect and the holds are dreamy. Every route is worthy, so do them all! You can climb this boulder year-round, however, summer afternoons are hot. Also, don't forget your pad, as there are a handful of excellent V6ish boulder problems.

To find this area, take the logging road from the **East Campground** towards the **Roman Wall**. Look to your left for the wooden sign.

1.   Monkeys on Magoo 5.10a ★★★
This is located on the south side of **Magoo Rock**. Start on the arête and move right. Climb large, strange holds to a small pod. Pull out of the pod on steep stone to good holds and anchors. (5 bolts) 55 ft.
FA: Chad Watkins '03

2.   Man Servant 5.9+ ★★★★
Start on **Monkeys on Magoo**, but stay on the left side of the arête. Climb good holds to a small roof. Pull over the roof onto a stance for the anchors. (5 bolts) 55 ft.
FA: Chad Watkins '03

3.   Road Hog 5.10a ★★★★
Start five feet left of the arête and climb straight up superb stone. (6 bolts) 55 ft.
FA: Chad Watkins '03

Magoo Rock • 79

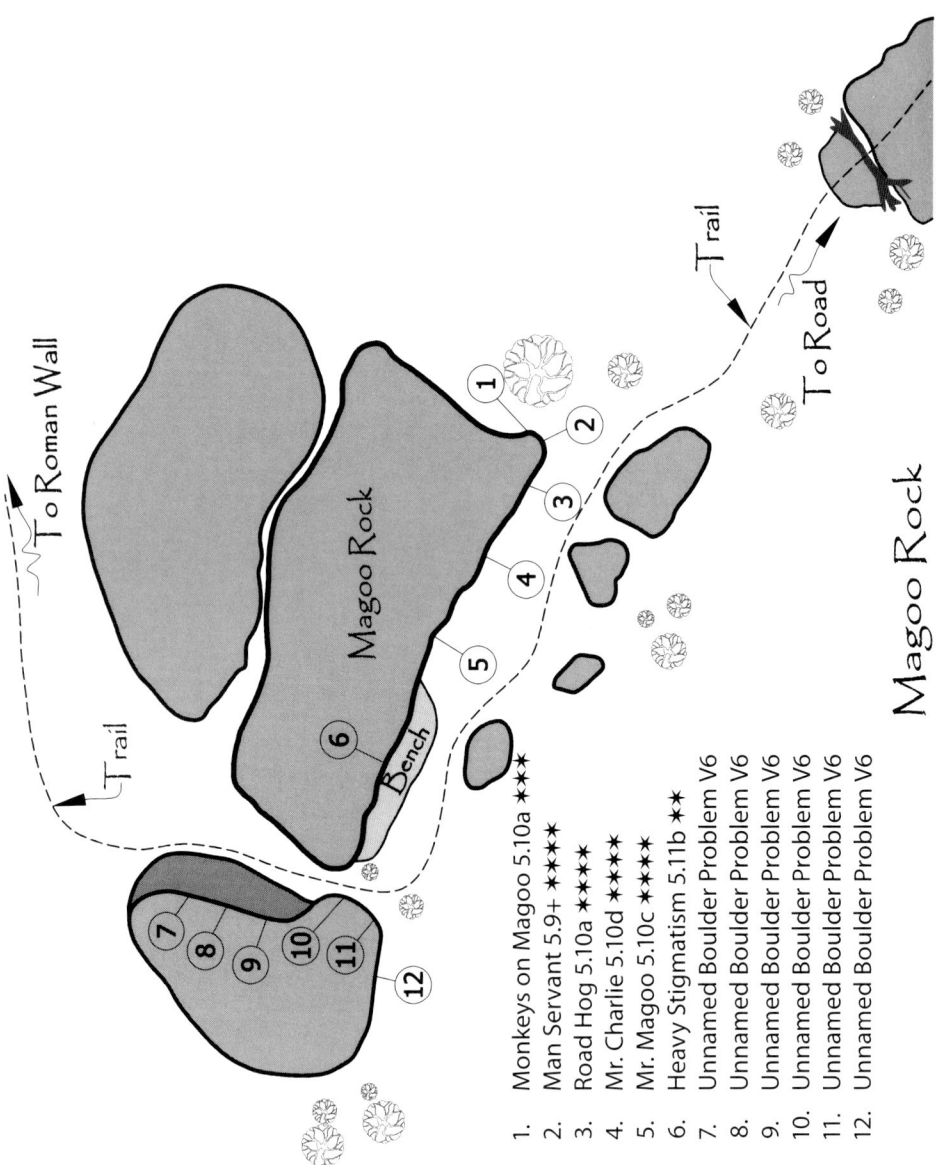

Another unknown Redbull Redpoint Roundup competitor on Mr. Charlie

4. **Mr. Charlie 5.10d** ✶✶✶✶
Ten feet left of **Road Hog**, start on small holds to make a long move to an undercling. Pull out of this onto jugs. Climb up to crimps and slightly right to more crimps and then up to a slanted roof. Move left below the roof to the edge. Pull up on pockets and jugs to reach a good stance at the anchors. (6 bolts) 55 ft.
FA: Chad Watkins '03

5. **Mr. Magoo 5.10c** ✶✶✶✶
Boulder into the shallow, white dihedral to make the first clip. A tough move allows you to step to a lieback flake. Climb through this and encounter some perfect holds (if you have not already). A tenuous move will land you at the anchors with a good clipping hold. (6 bolts) 55 ft.
FA: Chad Watkins '03

6. **Heavy Stigmatism 5.11b** ✶✶
Boulder up onto the ledge on the left to start this one. Start on decent holds and pull up to a thin lieback on crimps. Make a long reach left to a pocket and a crimp. Pull through this and climb jugs to the top. (4 bolts) 40 ft.
FA: Chad Watkins '03

Chad Watkins battles Maximus

ROMAN WALL

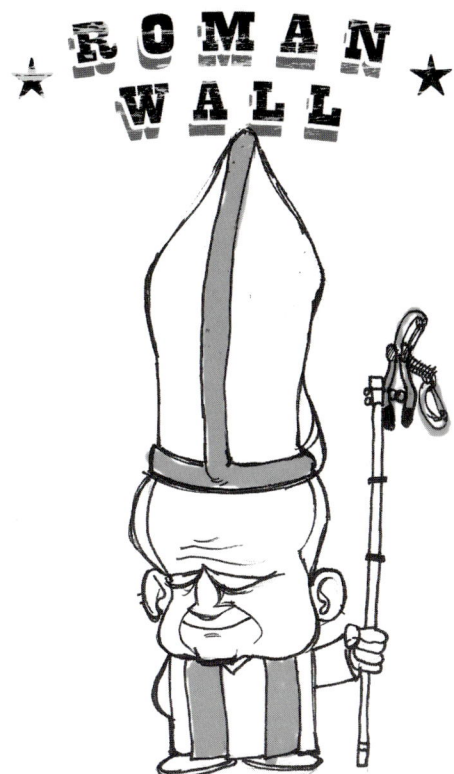

The **Roman Wall** is another popular spot, great in the winter for all-day cragging and good in the summer for the early birds. Don't try to climb here midday in the dead of summer, though, or you will bake. Even if its not summer, get there early; there have actually been people waiting in line to get on the routes here, and though there are not a lot of routes, they are all worth doing.

To find this area, take the logging road from the **East Campground** and hike southeasterly uphill through the trees. When you find the road again, turn right and continue to the trailhead marked by a wooden sign on a tree. At the top of the trail, stay left.

1. **Warthog 5.8 PG**
This is the juggy face climb on the wall left of and facing the **Roman Wall**. (trad w/ anchors) 55 ft.
FA: Chad Watkins '02

2. **Don't Be Gay 5.11b** ★★
At the left edge of the **Roman Wall**, start in the dihedral on the slab to the left. Climb the slab up to and on top of precarious plates and boulders. Steep, sustained climbing follows on good holds to anchors. (7 bolts) 65 ft.
FA: Mark Carter '02

3. **Commodus 5.10a** ★★★★
Start on either side of this superb arête and climb balancy moves to the top. (5 bolts) 45 ft.
FA: Chad Watkins '02

The infamous Rich McDade on Boronocus

4. Maximus 5.12b **

You can access this route by way of **Commodus**. Climb fixed draws to the top. Please do not steal the biners. (fixed) 80 ft.
FA: Rich McDade '02

5. Spartacus 5.11d **

Five feet right of **Commodus**, climb just right of the thin seam to steeper stone. A powerful undercling move puts you into the crux; move right, and then up. (4 bolts) 45 ft.
FA: Chad Watkins '02

6. Boronocus 5.11c **

Start this route ten feet right of **Spartacus** on jugs up to a stance. Sustained climbing on crimps takes you thirty-five feet to the break. Mantle onto the upper headwall and climb overhanging jugs and crimps to the roof. Then pull over the lip to a stance to reach the anchors. (11 bolts) 75 ft.
FA: Chad Watkins '02

7. Caesar's Tossed Salad 5.10c **

Start just right and climb good slopers and jugs to the break. Pull onto the upper headwall and climb crimps and jugs on excellent stone to a small break. Pull past this and into the crux to reach the anchors. (9 bolts) 75 ft.
FA: Chad Watkins '03

8. Sybarite 5.9 **

Start under a small roof and move left and then back right to pull over the roof. Continue on rounded jugs to the top. (5 bolts) 45 ft.
FA: Kerry Allen '02

9. Centurion 5.10a **

Climb the black stone up technical moves to jugs at the end. (6 bolts) 45 ft.
FA: Chad Watkins '03

10. Aphrodite 5.7 **

This climb is the jugfest at the right end of the wall. (5 bolts) 45 ft.
FA: Chad Watkins '02

Chandra Anderson on Caesar's Tossed Salad

Luke Stufflebeam climbing Little Sprout

Cliffs of Insanity

The **Cliffs of Insanity** are right next-door to the **Roman Wall** and are a great place for the novice climber. With both of these areas combined you have an excellent group of routes ranging from 5.6 to 5.12b.

To find this area, use the same directions as for the **Roman Wall**, but stay right at the top of the trail.

11. One Piece at a Time 5.7+
Climb the obvious wide crack. (trad w/o anchors) 60 ft.
FA: Unknown

12. Rubber Chicken 5.6 ★★★
Start on the boulder/bench on the left side of the wall. Some vertical climbing leads to slabby jug climbing further up. Try not to trip over the jugs. (7 bolts) 65 ft.
FA: Chad Watkins '02

13. Little Sprout 5.6 ★★★
Start down by the small tree on reachy moves up to jugs. Continue on jugs to the top. (7 bolts) 65 ft.
FA: Chad Watkins '02

14. Fesic 5.6 ★★
Start on **Little Sprout**, only move right and climb jugs to the top. (7 bolts) 65 ft.
FA: Chad Watkins '02

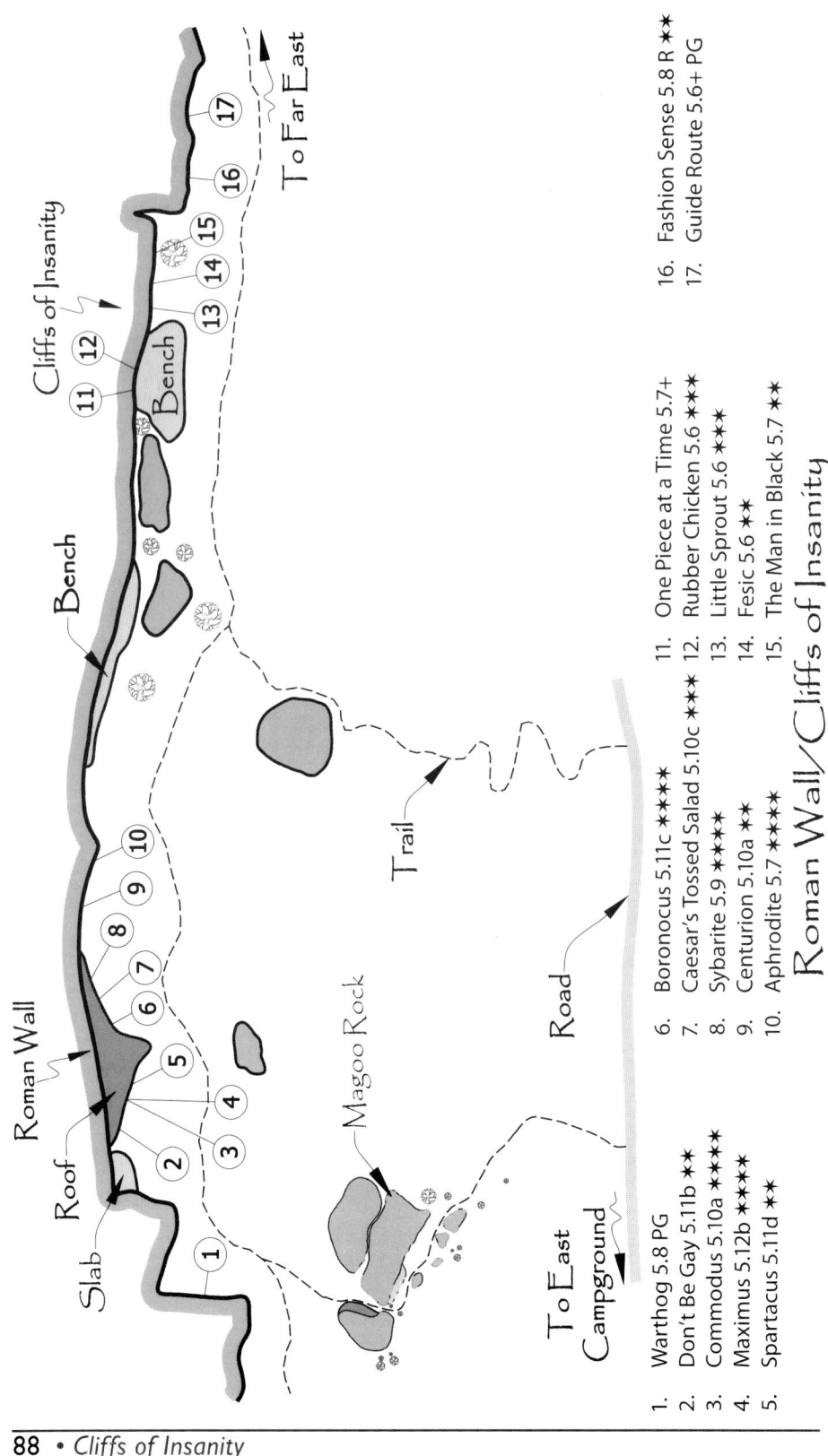

A Redbull Redpoint Roundup competitor on Spine Tingler

15. The Man in Black 5.7 ✶✶
Start twenty feet right of **Fesic** on a juggy ramp. Climb a bulge on jugs to a ledge. Continue on jugs to the top. (7 bolts) 65 ft.
FA: Chad Watkins '03

16. Fashion Sense 5.8 R ✶✶
Start twenty feet right of **The Man in Black**, past a bowling pin boulder, on a ramp. Begin at the high end of the ramp on small holds. Then climb jugs interspersed with the occasional slab move. (5 bolts) 65 ft.
FA: Chad Watkins '02

17. Guide Route 5.6+ PG
Further right, climb a juggy face to anchors half-way up. (trad w/anchors) 40 ft.
FA: Alf Carter

Matt Lyons at the crux mantle of Emotional Content

the FAR EAST

The **Far East** is a great area with a nice variety of both sport and trad climbs. There are a lot of good routes in this area so it's hard to pick the best ones. For cracks, **First Time Up** is a super line, with hand to fist jam climbing up a perfect flake. Further down the bluff, climb **Blood Brothers** for a spicier slice of 5.9+ flake climbing. For sport, your choices are many. **Orange Crush** holds the title for most bolts on the Ranch with 14 — most folks don't even have that many draws. **Emotional Content** is good for practicing your 5.10 mantling ability, while **Supersoul Sureshot** will surely test your 5.12 lunging ability. These are just a few and will not necessarily be the best, but you'll have to find that out for yourself. This area is shaded in spots and exposed in others, so summer can be good in the morning and hot in the afternoon. Winter, however, is the best time for all-day climbing.

To find this area, take the trail up to the **Roman Wall** and hang a right.

18. First Time Up 5.8+ ★★★★
Hike past the **Cliffs of Insanity** and around the corner. This is the perfect right-facing dihedral flake, with a classic hand/fist sized crack with good gear placements. (trad w/o anchors) 55 ft.
FA: Unknown

19. Gracie's Eight 5.8+ ★★★
Start just right of **First Time Up**. Climb moderate moves to steeper stone, negotiate the crux and continue to the anchors. (7 bolts) 55 ft.
FA: Chad Watkins '03

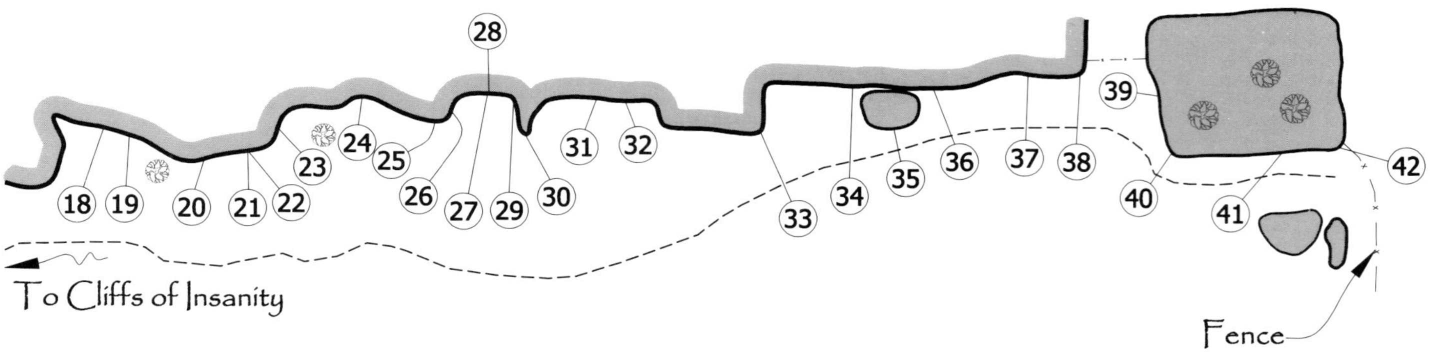

18. First Time Up 5.8+ ★★★★
19. Gracie's Eight 5.8+ ★★★
20. The Farrier 5.12a ★
21. Horseshoes and Hand Grenades 5.11a ★★★★
22. Cowgirl Up 5.9 PG ★★
23. Space Monkey 5.11c ★★★
24. Pills on an Empty Stomach 5.8+
25. Recidivist 5.10b ★★
26. Emotional Content 5.10b ★★★★
27. Manked 5.9- PG
28. Alesia 5.11a ★★★
29. King Kong 5.11a ★★★
30. Spine Tingler 5.12a ★★★
31. Bury the Boot 5.9+ ★
32. Tuff Gong 5.10d ★★
33. Filthy Sanchez 5.12a/b ★★★★
34. Blood Brothers 5.9 ★★★
35. Montezuma's Toe 5.8+ ★★★
36. Montezuma's Revenge 5.8+ ★
37. Pieces of Eight 5.11b/c ★★★★
38. September Hero 5.10b ★★★
39. Supersoul Sureshot 5.12c ★★★★
40. Plumb Bob 5.11b ★★★★
41. Purple Nehi 5.11c ★★★
42. Orange Crush 5.9+ ★★★★

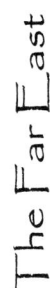

The Far East

20. The Farrier 5.12a ✶
Thirty feet right of **Gracie's Eight** is a thin dihedral. Climb strenuous moves to a blank section at the top of the dihedral. Move right to finish on **Horseshoes and Hand Grenades**. (6 bolts) 60 ft.
FA: Clay Frisbie '01

21. Horseshoes and Hand Grenades 5.11a ✶✶✶✶
A few feet right of **The Farrier**, climb this technical and fun route on beautiful stone. (8 bolts) 60 ft.
FA: Clay Frisbie '01

22. Cowgirl Up 5.9 PG ✶✶
Start at the base of **Horseshoes and Hand Grenades** and traverse right to the arête. Continue up the arete with easier climbing. (trad w/o anchors) 60 ft.
FA: Clay Frisbie '01

23. Space Monkey 5.11c ✶✶✶
Right of the arête, begin in the nook behind the large tree. Start with easy moves up the bulge right and move back left to climb thin, technical moves to the top. (7 bolts) 60 ft.
FA: Chad Watkins '02

24. Pills on an Empty Stomach 5.8+
To the right of **Space Monkey** lies a dirty fingers to hands crack in a dihedral. The top-out can leave one a bit queasy. (trad w/o anchors) 60 ft.
FA: Cina Canada '01

25. Recidivist 5.10b ✶✶
Right of the dihedral, climb the striking, blunt arête on orange stone. A difficult start leads to easier climbing above. (7 bolts) 60 ft.
FA: Chad Watkins '02

26. Emotional Content 5.10b ✶✶✶✶
Start in the dihedral and move left onto the face at the second bolt. Continue up and left to steeper stone, and mantle to reach the anchors. (7 bolts) 60 ft.
FA: Chad Watkins '02

27. Manked 5.9- PG
Start in the dihedral and climb the broken corner. (trad w/o anchors) 60 ft.
FA: Unknown

28. Alesia 5.11a ✶✶✶
Climb the route that suits you in the alcove to gain the cave above. Then climb the obvious roof via a large flake. (4 bolts) 40 ft.
FA: Roger Raines '04

29. King Kong 5.11a ✶✶✶
Start in the dihedral, and move right at the second bolt. Keep trending right and up on pumpy moves to the top . (8 bolts) 60 ft.
FA: Dave McGee '01

30. Spine Tingler 5.12a ✶✶✶
Climb crimps on either side of the striking fin to the roof. Pull out the roof to a stance on the slab. Easy climbing takes you to the top. (6 bolts) 55 ft.
FA: Chad Watkins '02

31. Bury the Boot 5.9+ ✶
Step around the corner right of **Spine Tingler** up the slope to a short wall. Climb the broken crack system to a splitter hand crack at the top. (trad w/o anchors) 40 ft.
FA: Clay Frisbie '01

Tom Hancock on Plumb Bob

Misty Lamb on September Hero

32. Tuff Gong 5.10d ★★
Right of the puddle, start on crimps and climb bouldery moves on good stone to a bulge. Pull over the bulge to reach the anchors. (5 bolts) 45 ft.
FA: Chad Watkins '02

33. Filthy Sanchez 5.12a/b ★★★★
Walk the trail fifty yards to a sharp, south-facing arête. Climb thin, delicate moves all the way up. Technical moves at the top guard the anchors. (7 bolts) 55 ft.
FA: Chad Watkins '02

34. Blood Brothers 5.9 ★★★
This superb, left-angling crack/flake with good gear is a must-do! (trad w/o anchors) 60 ft.
FA: Jeremy Collins '01

35. Montezuma's Toe 5.8+ ★★★
Climb the pillar on easy ground to more difficult moves at the top. (5 bolts) 40 ft.
FA: Jason Roy '02

36. Montezuma's Revenge 5.8+ ★
This is the wide crack with a tree in it just right of the pillar. (trad w/o anchors) 60 ft.
FA: Clay Frisbie '02

37. Pieces of Eight 5.11b/c ★★★★
Fifteen feet right of **Montezuma's Revenge**, start in a shallow dihedral in the face. Pull into the dihedral and reach to the top to find a good hold. From here, glide right onto the bulge using tiny holds. Continue up through several difficult moves past a large break to a stance before trending left to finish. (9 bolts) 60 ft.
FA: Chad Watkins '02

38. September Hero 5.10b ★★★
Start on the blunt arête on the main cliff just opposite of **Supersoul Sureshot**. Climb easy moves to gain a ledge. Pull onto the face above and find the rather formidable crux guarding the anchors. An attentive belay will keep you from hitting the ledge if you blow the clip at the anchors. (6 bolts) 60 ft.
FA: Jason Roy '02

39. Supersoul Sureshot 5.12c ★★★★
This is the brilliant steep face on the large boulder to the right of the fence. A boulder problem start leads to several long moves on jugs. (7 bolts) 60 ft.
FA: Chris Robertson '02

40. Plumb Bob 5.11b ★★★★
Drop down and right of **Supersoul Sureshot** to find the start of this overhanging arête on the right side of the large boulder. Climb the arête to the splitter crack above. (7 bolts) 60 ft.
FA: Chad Watkins '02

41. Purple Nehi 5.11c ★★★
This is just left of **Orange Crush** on the steep orange stone. Move through sustained climbing on crimps to the anchors. (11 bolts) 65 ft.
FA: Chad Watkins '02

42. Orange Crush 5.9+ ★★★★
Climb the obvious arête at the fence. Although this route has a lot of bolts, it does have a bit of a tricky section through the crux which has been the scene of more than one unplanned whipper. NOTE: A 60 METER ROPE IS REQUIRED. (14 bolts) 90 ft.
FA: Chad Watkins '02

Tick List

5.5

☐ Guide Route 5.5 ★★ 54, 57

5.6

☐ Cotton Candy 5.6 ★★★★ 46, 52
☐ Fesic 5.6 ★★ 87, 88
☐ Kid's Stuff 5.6 .... 54, 56
☐ Little Sprout 5.6 ★★★ 87, 88
☐ Missing Rack 5.6 ....46, 47
☐ Rubber Chicken 5.6 ★★★ 87, 88
☐ Webster's Part 5.6 ★★★ 54, 55

5.6+

☐ Guide Route 5.6+ PG 88, 89

5.7

☐ Aphrodite 5.7 ★★★★ 84, 88
☐ Cows in the Mist 5.7 ★★★ 54, 57
☐ Dancing Bears 5.7 ★★★ 46, 52
☐ The Elephant Man 5.7 ....46, 47
☐ Emma's Got a Mullet 5.7 ★★ 54, 57
☐ Flying Squirrel 5.7 .... 34, 35
☐ Girth Hitch 5.7 ★★★ 54, 55
☐ Little Manly Man 5.7 ★★ 54, 56
☐ The Man in Black 5.7 ★★ 88, 89
☐ Narwhal 5.7 ★ 54, 57
☐ Public Access 5.7 .... 24, 25
☐ Summer Rain 5.7 ★★★ 46, 52
☐ Sundial 5.7 ★★★ 54, 56
☐ Tequila Sunrise 5.7 ....76, 77
☐ Tunnel Vision 5.7 ★ 54, 56
☐ Up Yours Ashcroft 5.7 ★ 24, 29
☐ Wanted Man 5.7 .... 46, 52
☐ Zeppelin 5.7 .... 54, 56

5.7+

☐ One Piece at a Time 5.7+ 87, 88

5.8-

☐ Treebeard 5.8- ★★★ 24, 28

5.8

☐ Around the Fur 5.8 ★★★★ 46, 47
☐ Brand New 5.8 ★★ 54, 57
☐ The Bulb 5.8 ★★★ 54, 56
☐ Clown Suit 5.8 .... 54, 55
☐ Dirty Crack Whore 5.8 G ★★ 16, 17
☐ Earl's Revenge 5.8 ....46, 47
☐ Fashion Sense 5.8 R ★★ 88, 89
☐ Green Goblin 5.8 ★★★ 46, 51
☐ Groovy 5.8 ★★★ 54, 56
☐ Hickadelic Jazzgrass 5.8 PG ★★ ..15, 16
☐ Keep'em Separated 5.8 PG ★ 46, 48
☐ Lost Left Sock 5.8 ★★ 68, 71
☐ Product of Kush 5.8 ★★ 24, 28
☐ Ramblin' Man 5.8 ★★ 38, 39
☐ Right Hook of Allah 5.8 ★ PG 24, 26
☐ Tales of Ribaldry 5.8 ★ 24, 26
☐ Tres Equis 5.8 ★★★ 54, 56
☐ The Vegetable 5.8 PG 16, 17
☐ Warthog 5.8 PG 83, 88

5.8+

☐ African Herbman 5.8+ ★★★★ 54, 55
☐ Barley & Hops 5.8+ ★★ 15, 16
☐ First Time Up 5.8+ ★★★★ 91, 92
☐ Gracie's Eight 5.8+ ★★★ 91, 92
☐ The Greatest Show on Earth 5.8+
   ★★★★ 52, 54
☐ Groove Tube 5.8+ PG 54, 56
☐ Harry Butthole Pussy Potter 5.8+
   ★★★ 46, 47
☐ Kurbcheck 5.8+ ★★★ 46, 47
☐ Molt 5.8+ ★★★ 54, 56
☐ Montezuma's Revenge 5.8+ ★ ... 92, 95
☐ Montezuma's Toe 5.8+ ★★★ 92, 95
☐ Old School 5.8+ ★ 16, 17
☐ Party in the Back 5.8+ ★★★★ 68, 69
☐ Squirrel Deck 5.8+ ★★★ 42, 43

5.9-

- ☐ Circus Freaks 5.9- PG ★ 54, 55
- ☐ The Controversy 5.9- ★★ 46, 52
- ☐ Hackberry Crack 5.9- ★★★★★ 24, 28
- ☐ Jackhole 5.9- ★★ 46, 47
- ☐ Left Hook of God 5.9- ★ PG 24, 26
- ☐ Lion Tamer 5.9- ★★★★ 46, 52
- ☐ Local Hebrew 5.9- ★★★ 54, 56
- ☐ Manked 5.9- PG 92, 93

5.9

- ☐ Blood Brothers 5.9 ★★★ 92, 95
- ☐ Cowgirl Up 5.9 PG ★★ 92, 93
- ☐ Gilgamek Vagina 5.9 ★★ 24, 29
- ☐ I Fought Guppies 5.9 ★ 24, 25
- ☐ Lamb Chops 5.9 PG 54, 55
- ☐ Poetry in Goshen 5.9 PG 54, 55
- ☐ Rosie's Cantina 5.9 ★ 76, 77
- ☐ Side Show 5.9 PG ★ 46, 52
- ☐ Sybarite 5.9 ★★★★ 84, 88
- ☐ Whiskey River 5.9 PG ★★★ 68, 71

5.9+

- ☐ Breach 5.9+ PG ★★ 42, 43
- ☐ Bury the Boot 5.9+ ★ 92, 93
- ☐ The Catholic Boat 5.9+ ★★★ 16, 18
- ☐ Deft Jam 5.9+ ★★★ 23, 24
- ☐ Entwash 5.9+ ★ 24, 26
- ☐ First Normal Form 5.9+ ★★★ 46, 51
- ☐ Frankenberry 5.9+ 46, 52
- ☐ Hand Grenade 5.9+ ★ 16, 18
- ☐ Karkaras 5.9+ PG ★ 46, 48
- ☐ Leonid 5.9+ ★★★ 54, 55
- ☐ The Lookout 5.9+ ★★ 42, 43
- ☐ Man Servant 5.9+ ★★★★ 79, 80
- ☐ Mortar Fire 5.9+ ★★ 16, 18
- ☐ Solid 5.9+ ★★★ 24, 26
- ☐ Stem Cell Research 5.9+ ★ 24, 26
- ☐ Strongman 5.9+ ★★★★ 46, 52
- ☐ W.M.A. 5.9+ ★★★★ 24, 25
- ☐ The Wet One 5.9+ PG 24, 29
- ☐ When Mullets Attack 5.9+ R ★★ 68, 69

5.10a

- ☐ Ask Dr. Stupid 5.10a ★★★ 34, 35
- ☐ Centurion 5.10a ★★ 84, 88
- ☐ Commodus 5.10a ★★★★ 83, 88
- ☐ Count Chalkula 5.10a ★★ 46, 52
- ☐ Gimp and Wheezer 5.10a ★★★★ 24, 26
- ☐ Message to Hairy Back Man 5.10a ★★ 24, 28
- ☐ Military Cut 5.10a ★★★ 68, 69
- ☐ Mohawk 5.10a ★★ 68, 69
- ☐ Monkeys on Magoo 5.10a ★★★ . 79, 80
- ☐ Private Property 5.10a ★★★ 54, 55
- ☐ Road Hog 5.10a ★★★★ 79, 80
- ☐ The Seamstress 5.10a ★★★ 24, 28
- ☐ Shelob's Lair 5.10a PG 24, 28
- ☐ Sons of the Soil 5.10a ★★ 54, 56
- ☐ Sour Girl 5.10a ★★★ 45, 46
- ☐ Stove Top 5.10a ★★★ 24, 26
- ☐ Up Your Buttress 5.10a ★★★ 24, 25

5.10b

- ☐ Business in the Front 5.10b ★★★ 68, 69
- ☐ Camaro Mullet 5.10b ★★ 68, 69
- ☐ Emotional Content 5.10b ★★★★ 92, 93
- ☐ Hasenpfeffer 5.10b ★★★★ 16, 17
- ☐ Hiking Under the Influence 5.10b ★★★ 68, 73
- ☐ Jihad 5.10b ★★ 38, 39
- ☐ Log 5.10b ★★ 34, 35
- ☐ More Better 5.10b ★★★ 46, 48
- ☐ Recidivist 5.10b ★★ 92, 93
- ☐ September Hero 5.10b ★★★ 92, 95

5.10c

- ☐ Caesar's Tossed Salad 5.10c ★★★ 84, 88
- ☐ Captain Disco 5.10c ★★ 16, 17
- ☐ Full Frontal Nudity 5.10c ★★★ 67, 68
- ☐ Ignatius 5.10c PG ★★★ 67, 68
- ☐ Knob Creek 5.10c ★★★★ 24, 28
- ☐ Learning to Fly 5.10c ★★★★ 38, 39
- ☐ Mad Man with an Afro 5.10c ★ ... 24, 25
- ☐ Mini-Me 5.10c ★★ 68, 73
- ☐ Mr. Magoo 5.10c ★★★★ 80, 81

5.10d

- ☐ Anal Sac Expression 5.10d ★★★ . 62, 63
- ☐ Crimp Scampi 5.10d ★★★★ 54, 55
- ☐ Devil's Candy 5.10d ★★★ 24, 26
- ☐ Fat Bastard 5.10d ★★ 24, 25
- ☐ In The Crack or On Your Back 5.10d
  ★★★★ 24, 29
- ☐ Meatcake 5.10d ★★★ 16, 17
- ☐ Mr. Charlie 5.10d ★★★★ 80, 81
- ☐ Mr. Hanky 5.10d ★★ 54, 55
- ☐ Port Side 5.10d ★★★★ 42, 43
- ☐ T-Rex 5.10d ★★★★ 16, 18
- ☐ Troubadour 5.10d ★★★★ 67, 68
- ☐ Tuff Gong 5.10d ★★ 92, 95
- ☐ Unnamed 5.10d ★★ 24, 28

5.11a

- ☐ Alesia 5.11a ★★★ 92, 93
- ☐ Bearded Lady 5.11a PG ★★ 46, 48
- ☐ Classique 5.11a ★★★★ 16, 18
- ☐ Cracked Rib 5.11a ★★ 41, 42
- ☐ Horny Goatweed 5.11a ★★ 46, 47
- ☐ Horseshoes and Hand Grenades 5.11a
  ★★★★ 92, 93
- ☐ King Kong 5.11a ★★★ 92, 93
- ☐ Milquetoast 5.11a ★★ 16, 17
- ☐ Newton County Mentality 5.11a
  ★★★ 54, 57
- ☐ Pimp-Ass Midgiemullet 5.11a
  ★★★ 68, 69
- ☐ Starboard List 5.11a ★★★ 41, 42

5.11a/b

- ☐ Mexican Sac Pull 5.11a/b ★★★★   62, 63
- ☐ PBR 5.11a/b ★★★★ 62, 63

5.11b

- ☐ Big Top 5.11b ★★★★ 46, 51
- ☐ Brass in Pocket 5.11b R 46, 51
- ☐ Chinese Soul Food 5.11b ★★★ 24, 25
- ☐ Don't Be Gay 5.11b ★★ 83, 88
- ☐ Electroglide 5.11b ★★★ 16, 17
- ☐ Fighting Uruk-hai 5.11b ★★★ 24, 26
- ☐ Heavy Stigmatism 5.11b ★★ 80, 81
- ☐ Plumb Bob 5.11b ★★★★ 92, 95
- ☐ The Poo-Choo Train 5.11b ★★ 75, 76
- ☐ Sonny Jim 5.11b ★★★★ 46, 48
- ☐ Tattooed Lady 5.11b ★★★ 46, 48
- ☐ The Mud, The Blood & The Beer 5.11a
  ★★★ 23, 24

5.11b/c

- ☐ Mountain Meadow Massacre 5.11b/c
  PG ★ 24, 25
- ☐ Pieces of Eight 5.11b/c ★★★★ 92, 95

5.11c

- ☐ Balrog 5.11c ★★ 24, 26
- ☐ Boronocus 5.11c ★★★★ 84, 88
- ☐ I Fought Piranhas 5.11c ★★★ 24, 25
- ☐ Newton's Law 5.11c ★★★ 24, 28
- ☐ Purple Nehi 5.11c ★★★ 92, 95
- ☐ Space Monkey 5.11c ★★★ 92, 93

5.11d

- ☐ Elephant Ear 5.11d ★★★ 16, 17
- ☐ Frogger 5.11d ★★★ 24, 26
- ☐ Mixed Max 5.11d ★★ 67, 68
- ☐ Serfs and Lords 5.11d ★★ 46, 48
- ☐ Spartacus 5.11d ★★ 84, 88
- ☐ Taliban Soup 5.11d ★★★★ 38, 39
- ☐ Trapeze Artist 5.11d ★ 46, 51

5.11d/12a

- ☐ Space Madness 5.11d/12a ★★★ .. 33, 34

5.12a

- ☐ Atlantis 5.12a ★★★ 68, 72
- ☐ Austrian Ass Attack 5.12a ★★★★ 62, 63
- ☐ Don't Be A Tool 5.12a ★★★ 75, 76
- ☐ Door Prize 5.12a ★★ 24, 25
- ☐ The Farrier 5.12a ★ 92, 93
- ☐ Granny Tranny 5.12a ★★ 37, 38
- ☐ Greasy Kid's Stuff 5.12a ★★ 62, 63
- ☐ Lavender Eye 5.12a ★★★★ 46, 51
- ☐ Love Slave 5.12a ★★ 46, 47
- ☐ Mine, Mine, Mine 5.12a ★★★ 46, 47
- ☐ The Penny Cigarette 5.12a ★★★ . 68, 72
- ☐ Petrified 5.12a ★★ 54, 55
- ☐ Spine Tingler 5.12a ★★★ 92, 93

5.12a/b

- ☐ Crab Louse 5.12a/b PG ★ 54, 57
- ☐ 420 5.12a/b ★★★ 16, 17
- ☐ Fat Hand 5.12a/b ★★★★ 46, 51
- ☐ Filthy Sanchez 5.12a/b ★★★★ 92, 95

5.12b

- ☐ The Big Sleep 5.12b ★★★ 33, 34
- ☐ Bum Fight 5.12b ★★★ 76, 77
- ☐ The Gigolo 5.12b ★★★★ 16, 18
- ☐ Jimmy Hoffa 5.12b ★★★ 68, 72
- ☐ Junk Bus 5.12b ★★★ 62, 63
- ☐ Man Junk 5.12b ★★★★ 62, 63
- ☐ Maximus 5.12b ★★★★ 84, 88
- ☐ Nova Monkey 5.12b ★★★★ 24, 29
- ☐ Powdered Toast Man 5.12b
  ★★★★ 34, 35
- ☐ Pride 5.12b ★★ 68, 72
- ☐ Ride the Short Bus 5.12b ★★★ 62, 64
- ☐ Sissy-made Training Academy 5.12b
  ★ 24, 29
- ☐ Sleestack 5.12b ★★★ 68, 72
- ☐ Strong Men Also Cry 5.12b ★★ 16, 18
- ☐ Tiny Bubbles 5.12b ★★ 24, 28
- ☐ Toxic Dementia 5.12b ★★★ 24, 28
- ☐ Wave 5.12b ★★ 16, 19

5.12b/c

- ☐ Dirty Trip 5.12b/c ★★ 62, 63
- ☐ Introrectogestion 5.12b/c ★★★ ..16, 18

5.12c

- ☐ Balooga 5.12c ★★★ 46, 48
- ☐ Corn Grinder 5.12c ★★★★ 46, 51
- ☐ Respect My Authority 5.12c
  ★★★★ 62, 64
- ☐ Shits and Giggles 5.12c ★ 61, 62
- ☐ Supersoul Sureshot 5.12c ★★★★ 92, 95
- ☐ Tsunami 5.12c ★★ 16, 18
- ☐ White Trash Took My Heavy Metal 5.12c
  ★★★ 16, 17

5.12c/d

- ☐ Egyptian Airbus 5.12c/d ★★★★ .. 38, 39
- ☐ Flabby Armed Spanking Machine
  5.12c/d ★★★★ 62, 64

5.12d

- ☐ Crockostimpy 5.12d ★★★★ 33, 34
- ☐ Johnny Revelator 5.12d ★★★ 46, 48
- ☐ XXX 5.12d ★ 24, 29

5.13a

- ☐ Envy 5.13a ★★ 68, 72
- ☐ Roary Breaker 5.13a ★★ 24, 25

5.13b

- ☐ Cradle of the Deep 5.13 ★★★★ 42, 43
- ☐ Venus Butterfly 5.13b ★★★★ 46, 48

5.13c

- ☐ U235 5.13? 16, 18

5.13d/14a

- ☐ The Prophet 5.13d/14a ★★★★ 37, 38

Tick List • 99

Route Index

A

- African Herbman 5.8+ ★★★★ 54, 55
- Alesia 5.11a ★★★ 92, 93
- Anal Sac Expression 5.10d ★★★ . 62, 63
- Aphrodite 5.7 ★★★★ 84, 88
- Around the Fur 5.8 ★★★★ 46, 47
- Ask Dr. Stupid 5.10a ★★★ 34, 35
- Atlantis 5.12a ★★★ 68, 72
- Austrian Ass Attack 5.12a ★★★★ 62, 63

B

- Balooga 5.12c ★★★ 46, 48
- Balrog 5.11c ★★ 24, 26
- Barley & Hops 5.8+ ★★ 15, 16
- Bearded Lady 5.11a PG ★★ 46, 48
- The Big Sleep 5.12b ★★★ 33, 34
- Big Top 5.11b ★★★★ 46, 51
- Blood Brothers 5.9 ★★★ 92, 95
- Boronocus 5.11c ★★★★ 84, 88
- Brand New 5.8 ★★ 54, 57
- Brass in Pocket 5.11b R 46, 51
- Breach 5.9+ PG ★★ 42, 43
- The Bulb 5.8 ★★★ 54, 56
- Bum Fight 5.12b ★★★ 76, 77
- Bury the Boot 5.9+ ★ 92, 93
- Business in the Front 5.10b ★★★ 68, 69

C

- Caesar's Tossed Salad 5.10c ★★★ 84, 88
- Camaro Mullet 5.10b ★★ 68, 69
- Captain Disco 5.10c ★★ 16, 17
- The Catholic Boat 5.9+ ★★★ 16, 18
- Centurion 5.10a ★★ 84, 88
- Chinese Soul Food 5.11b ★★★ 24, 25
- Circus Freaks 5.9- PG ★ 54, 55
- Classique 5.11a ★★★★ 16, 18
- Clown Suit 5.8 .... 54, 55
- Commodus 5.10a ★★★★ 83, 88
- The Controversy 5.9- ★★ 46, 52
- Corn Grinder 5.12c ★★★★ 46, 51
- Cotton Candy 5.6 ★★★★ 46, 52
- Count Chalkula 5.10a ★★ 46, 52
- Cowgirl Up 5.9 PG ★★ 92, 93
- Cows in the Mist 5.7 ★★★ 54, 57
- Crab Louse 5.12a/b PG ★ 54, 57
- Cracked Rib 5.11a ★★ 41, 42
- Cradle of the Deep 5.13 ★★★★ 42, 43
- Crimp Scampi 5.10d ★★★★ 54, 55
- Crockostimpy 5.12d ★★★★ 33, 34

D

- Dancing Bears 5.7 ★★★ 46, 52
- Deft Jam 5.9+ ★★★ 23, 24
- Devil's Candy 5.10d ★★★ 24, 26
- Dirty Crack Whore 5.8 G ★★ 16, 17
- Dirty Trip 5.12b/c ★★ 62, 63
- Don't Be A Tool 5.12a ★★★ 75, 76
- Don't Be Gay 5.11b ★★ 83, 88
- Door Prize 5.12a ★★ 24, 25

E

- Earl's Revenge 5.8 .... 46, 47
- Egyptian Airbus 5.12c/d ★★★★ .. 38, 39
- Electroglide 5.11b ★★★ 16, 17
- Elephant Ear 5.11d ★★★ 16, 17
- The Elephant Man 5.7 .... 46, 47
- Emma's Got a Mullet 5.7 ★★ 54, 57
- Emotional Content 5.10b ★★★★ 92, 93
- Entwash 5.9+ ★ 24, 26
- Envy 5.13a ★★ 68, 72

F

- 420 5.12a/b ★★★ 16, 17
- The Farrier 5.12a ★ 92, 93
- Fashion Sense 5.8 R ★★ 88, 89
- Fat Bastard 5.10d ★★ 24, 25
- Fat Hand 5.12a/b ★★★★ 46, 51
- Fesic 5.6 ★★ 87, 88
- Fighting Uruk-hai 5.11b ★★★ 24, 26
- Filthy Sanchez 5.12a/b ★★★★ 92, 95
- First Normal Form 5.9+ ★★★ 46, 51
- First Time Up 5.8+ ★★★★ 91, 92
- Flabby Armed Spanking Machine 5.12c/d ★★★★ 62, 64
- Flying Squirrel 5.7 .... 34, 35
- Frankenberry 5.9+ 46, 52

100 • Route Index

G

- ☐ Frogger 5.11d ★★★ 24, 26
- ☐ Full Frontal Nudity 5.10c ★★★ 67, 68

G

- ☐ The Gigolo 5.12b ★★★★ 16, 18
- ☐ Gilgamek Vagina 5.9 ★★ 24, 29
- ☐ Gimp and Wheezer 5.10a ★★★★ 24, 26
- ☐ Girth Hitch 5.7 ★★★ 54, 55
- ☐ Gracie's Eight 5.8+ ★★★ 91, 92
- ☐ Granny Tranny 5.12a ★★ 37, 38
- ☐ Greasy Kid's Stuff 5.12a ★★ 62, 63
- ☐ The Greatest Show on Earth 5.8+ ★★★★ 52, 54
- ☐ Green Goblin 5.8 ★★★ 46, 51
- ☐ Groove Tube 5.8+ PG 54, 56
- ☐ Groovy 5.8 ★★★ 54, 56
- ☐ Guide Route 5.5 ★★ 54, 57
- ☐ Guide Route 5.6+ PG 88, 89

H

- ☐ Hackberry Crack 5.9- ★★★★★ 24, 28
- ☐ Hand Grenade 5.9+ ★ 16, 18
- ☐ Harry Butthole Pussy Potter 5.8+ ★★★ 46, 47
- ☐ Hasenpfeffer 5.10b ★★★★ 16, 17
- ☐ Heavy Stigmatism 5.11b ★★ 80, 81
- ☐ Hickadelic Jazzgrass 5.8 PG ★★ .. 15, 16
- ☐ Hiking Under the Influence 5.10b ★★★ 68, 73
- ☐ Horny Goatweed 5.11a ★★ 46, 47
- ☐ Horseshoes and Hand Grenades 5.11a ★★★★ 92, 93

I

- ☐ I Fought Guppies 5.9 ★ 24, 25
- ☐ I Fought Piranhas 5.11c ★★★ 24, 25
- ☐ Ignatius 5.10c PG ★★★ 67, 68
- ☐ In The Crack or On Your Back 5.10d ★★★★ 24, 29
- ☐ Introrectogestion 5.12b/c ★★★ ... 16, 18

J

- ☐ Jackhole 5.9- ★★ 46, 47
- ☐ Jihad 5.10b ★★ 38, 39
- ☐ Jimmy Hoffa 5.12b ★★★ 68, 72

- ☐ Johnny Revelator 5.12d ★★★ 46, 48
- ☐ Junk Bus 5.12b ★★★ 62, 63

K

- ☐ Karkaras 5.9+ PG ★ 46, 48
- ☐ Keep'em Separated 5.8 PG ★ 46, 48
- ☐ Kid's Stuff 5.6 .... 54, 56
- ☐ Killing With Stone V6 .... 68, 72
- ☐ King Kong 5.11a ★★★ 92, 93
- ☐ Knob Creek 5.10c ★★★★ 24, 28
- ☐ Kurbcheck 5.8+ ★★★ 46, 47

L

- ☐ Lamb Chops 5.9 PG 54, 55
- ☐ Lavender Eye 5.12a ★★★★ 46, 51
- ☐ Learning to Fly 5.10c ★★★★ 38, 39
- ☐ Left Hook of God 5.9- ★ PG 24, 26
- ☐ Leonid 5.9+ ★★★ 54, 55
- ☐ Lion Tamer 5.9- ★★★★ 46, 52
- ☐ Little Manly Man 5.7 ★★ 54, 56
- ☐ Little Sprout 5.6 ★★★ 87, 88
- ☐ Local Hebrew 5.9- ★★★ 54, 56
- ☐ Log 5.10b ★★ 34, 35
- ☐ The Lookout 5.9+ ★★ 42, 43
- ☐ Lost Left Sock 5.8 ★★ 68, 71
- ☐ Love Slave 5.12a ★★ 46, 47

M

- ☐ Mad Man with an Afro 5.10c ★ ... 24, 25
- ☐ The Man in Black 5.7 ★★ 88, 89
- ☐ Man Junk 5.12b ★★★★ 62, 63
- ☐ Manked 5.9- PG 92, 93
- ☐ Man Servant 5.9+ ★★★★ 79, 80
- ☐ Maximus 5.12b ★★★★ 84, 88
- ☐ Meatcake 5.10d ★★★ 16, 17
- ☐ Message to Hairy Back Man 5.10a ★★ 24, 28
- ☐ Mexican Sac Pull 5.11a/b ★★★★ 62, 63
- ☐ Military Cut 5.10a ★★★ 68, 69
- ☐ Milquetoast 5.11a ★★ 16, 17
- ☐ Mine, Mine, Mine 5.12a ★★★★ ... 46, 47
- ☐ Mini-Me 5.10c ★★ 68, 73
- ☐ Missing Rack 5.6 .... 46, 47
- ☐ Mixed Max 5.11d ★★ 67, 68
- ☐ Mohawk 5.10a ★★ 68, 69
- ☐ Molt 5.8+ ★★★ 54, 56

Route Index • 101

- ☐ Monkeys on Magoo 5.10a ★★★ . 79, 80
- ☐ Montezuma's Revenge 5.8+ ★ ... 92, 95
- ☐ Montezuma's Toe 5.8+ ★★★ 92, 95
- ☐ More Better 5.10b ★★★ 46, 48
- ☐ Mortar Fire 5.9+ ★★ 16, 18
- ☐ Mountain Meadow Massacre 5.11b/c PG ★ 24, 25
- ☐ Mr. Charlie 5.10d ★★★★ 80, 81
- ☐ Mr. Hanky 5.10d ★★ 54, 55
- ☐ Mr. Magoo 5.10c ★★★★ 80, 81

N

- ☐ Narwhal 5.7 ★ 54, 57
- ☐ Newton's Law 5.11c ★★★ 24, 28
- ☐ Newton County Mentality 5.11a ★★★ 54, 57
- ☐ Nova Monkey 5.12b ★★★★ 24, 29

O

- ☐ Old School 5.8+ ★ 16, 17
- ☐ One Piece at a Time 5.7+ 87, 88

P

- ☐ Party in the Back 5.8+ ★★★★ 68, 69
- ☐ PBR 5.11a/b ★★★★ 62, 63
- ☐ The Penny Cigarette 5.12a ★★★ . 68, 72
- ☐ Petrified 5.12a ★★ 54, 55
- ☐ Pieces of Eight 5.11b/c ★★★★ 92, 95
- ☐ Pimp-Ass Midgiemullet 5.11a ★★★ 68, 69
- ☐ Plumb Bob 5.11b ★★★★ 92, 95
- ☐ Poetry in Goshen 5.9 PG 54, 55
- ☐ The Poo-Choo Train 5.11b ★★ 75, 76
- ☐ Port Side 5.10d ★★★★ 42, 43
- ☐ Powdered Toast Man 5.12b ★★★★ 34, 35
- ☐ Pride 5.12b ★★ 68, 72
- ☐ Private Property 5.10a ★★★ 54, 55
- ☐ Product of Kush 5.8 ★★ 24, 28
- ☐ The Prophet 5.13d/14a ★★★★ 37, 38
- ☐ Public Access 5.7 .... 24, 25
- ☐ Purple Nehi 5.11c ★★★ 92, 95

R

- ☐ Ramblin' Man 5.8 ★★ 38, 39
- ☐ Recidivist 5.10b ★★ 92, 93
- ☐ Respect My Authority 5.12c ★★★★ 62, 64
- ☐ Ride the Short Bus 5.12b ★★★ 62, 64
- ☐ Right Hook of Allah 5.8 ★ PG 24, 26
- ☐ Road Hog 5.10a ★★★★ 79, 80
- ☐ Roary Breaker 5.13a ★★ 24, 25
- ☐ Rosie's Cantina 5.9 ★ 76, 77
- ☐ Rubber Chicken 5.6 ★★★ 87, 88

S

- ☐ The Seamstress 5.10a ★★★ 24, 28
- ☐ September Hero 5.10b ★★★ 92, 95
- ☐ Serfs and Lords 5.11d ★★ 46, 48
- ☐ Shelob's Lair 5.10a PG 24, 28
- ☐ Shits and Giggles 5.12c ★ 61, 62
- ☐ Side Show 5.9 PG ★ 46, 52
- ☐ Sissy-made Training Academy 5.12b ★ 24, 29
- ☐ Sleestack 5.12b ★★★ 68, 72
- ☐ Solid 5.9+ ★★★ 24, 26
- ☐ Sonny Jim 5.11b ★★★★ 46, 48
- ☐ Sons of the Soil 5.10a ★★ 54, 56
- ☐ Sour Girl 5.10a ★★★ 45, 46
- ☐ Space Madness 5.11d/12a ★★★ .. 33, 34
- ☐ Space Monkey 5.11c ★★★ 92, 93
- ☐ Spartacus 5.11d ★★ 84, 88
- ☐ Spine Tingler 5.12a ★★★ 92, 93
- ☐ Squirrel Deck 5.8+ ★★★ 42, 43
- ☐ Starboard List 5.11a ★★★ 41, 42
- ☐ Stem Cell Research 5.9+ ★ 24, 26
- ☐ Stove Top 5.10a ★★★ 24, 26
- ☐ Strongman 5.9+ ★★★★ 46, 52
- ☐ Strong Men Also Cry 5.12b ★★ 16, 18
- ☐ Stuck in the Middle V6 .... 68, 72
- ☐ Summer Rain 5.7 ★★★ 46, 52
- ☐ Sundial 5.7 ★★★ 54, 56
- ☐ Supersoul Sureshot 5.12c ★★★★ 92, 95
- ☐ Sybarite 5.9 ★★★★ 84, 88

T

- ☐ T-Rex 5.10d ★★★★ 16, 18
- ☐ Tales of Ribaldry 5.8 ★ 24, 26
- ☐ Taliban Soup 5.11d ★★★★ 38, 39
- ☐ Tattooed Lady 5.11b ★★★ 46, 48
- ☐ Tequila Sunrise 5.7 .... 76, 77
- ☐ The Mud, The Blood & The Beer 5.11b ★★★ 23, 24
- ☐ Tiny Bubbles 5.12b ★★ 24, 28
- ☐ Tongue Lash V4 ★★★ 68, 69
- ☐ Toxic Dementia 5.12b ★★★ 24, 28
- ☐ Trapeze Artist 5.11d ★ 46, 51
- ☐ Treebeard 5.8- ★★★ 24, 28
- ☐ Tres Equis 5.8 ★★★ 54, 56
- ☐ Troubadour 5.10d ★★★★ 67, 68
- ☐ Tsunami 5.12c ★★ 16, 18
- ☐ Tuff Gong 5.10d ★★ 92, 95
- ☐ Tunnel Vision 5.7 ★ 54, 56

U

- ☐ U235 5.13? 16, 18
- ☐ Unnamed 5.10d ★★ 24, 28
- ☐ Up Your Buttress 5.10a ★★★ 24, 25
- ☐ Up Yours Ashcroft 5.7 ★ 24, 29

V

- ☐ The Vegetable 5.8 PG 16, 17
- ☐ Venus Butterfly 5.13b ★★★★ 46, 48

W

- ☐ W.M.A. 5.9+ ★★★★ 24, 25
- ☐ Wanted Man 5.7 .... 46, 52
- ☐ Warthog 5.8 PG 83, 88
- ☐ Wave 5.12b ★★ 16, 19
- ☐ Webster's Part 5.6 ★★★ 54, 55
- ☐ The Wet One 5.9+ PG 24, 29
- ☐ When Mullets Attack 5.9+ R ★★ 68, 69
- ☐ Whiskey River 5.9 PG ★★★ 68, 71
- ☐ White Trash Took My Heavy Metal 5.12c ★★★ 16, 17

X

- ☐ XXX 5.12d ★ 24, 29

Z

- ☐ Zeppelin 5.7 .... 54, 56

Notes

Please do not provoke the fearsome Anatolian poodle